Dyes from Kitchen Produce
Easy projects to make at home

SETSUKO ISHII

PHOTOGRAPHS BY MAKOTO SHIMOMURA

Teas...spices...garden herbs...
Many things available in the home can be used
for quick and easy dyeing.
This book contains all sorts of ideas suited to the seasons
of the year, for dyeing leftover fabrics and yarns and
making attractive, handy novelties.

contents

Kitchen Dyeing for Spring

Kitchen Dyeing for Summer

calendar
Twelve months in the house and garden

March	April	May	June	July	August
			June 8th Prune herbs before rainy season. Use stems for cuttings.		August 9th to 11th Prune herbs. Use some fresh cuttings for dyeing. Some I hang up to dry.
March 2nd Prepare soil in the garden. Plant seedlings 2 weeks later.		May 28th Make rose jam. 200 g of crimson rose petals and 100 g of sugar.		July 22nd Rainy season ends. Pick indigo in my mother's garden. Use the fresh leaves to dye wool.	
	April 18th The year's first crop. Fresh-picked herbs for herb tea and salad.				

Kitchen Dyeing for Autumn

Kitchen Dyeing for Winter

September	October	November	December	January	February
			December 5th Plant viola seeds. Prepare garden for winter.		February 8th Wash cotton fabrics to remove starch.
September 12th Make Japanese cakes with sweet chestnuts. Try dyeing with the cooking water.		November 17th Take my dog to the highlands. Collect foliage, vines and rose hips for seasonal wreaths.		January 12th Sort out wools and yarns ready for dyeing.	
	October 1st to 9th Prune herbs. Replant some, and sow more seeds. Sort out dried herbs.				

3

The Kitchen Dyeing Lifestyle

I discovered dyeing with herbs at a time when I was keen on gardening and was reading up on ways of using herbs. I'd used tea for dyeing lace to give it an antique look, but I'd never thought of making use of the trimmings from herbs, which grow so fast and need constant pruning. I first tried dyeing some ribbon with chamomile, using burnt alum as a mordant. Over the ten years since, I've thoroughly enjoyed trying out different dyes, wondering what sort of color I would get and watching it magically appear.

My first priority for dyeing is simplicity. I use what I have available, and dye things in my kitchen whenever an idea occurs to me. The house fills with the aroma of tea or the fresh fragrance of herbs. I gaze at the wonderful new color of a dyed fabric and think how best to use it and what to make it into. With the addition of kitchen dyeing, it's exciting to see all sorts of long-forgotten fabrics and yarns take on a new lease of life. I'm happy that I can enjoy making for myself a wide range of items for my home through easy, stress-free dyeing.

Lemongrass jelly for dessert

Flowers from the garden make a bouquet

A stock of test-dyed embroidery threads

I always serve herb tea to visitors

Fabric remnants and yarns can easily be dyed in a pan

Items for dyeing and resources to dye with, all found at home.

It doesn't matter if you don't have a garden because plenty of vegetables can also be used for dyeing. Tidy your kitchen shelves and see what else you can find. Tea and coffee, herb teas, health teas, dried mushrooms, spices... Once past their use-by date, they are all ideal for dyeing. Frozen blueberries you keep for desserts are good too. Spinach, purple cabbage and other leafy vegetables can be used, but I prefer to eat them! When you're cooking, keep the water after boiling black soybeans, adzuki beans or sweet chestnuts—it can be used just as it is as a great dyeing solution. Never throw away the skins or peelings of onions, mandarin oranges, grapes, peanuts, or pomegranates. Keep them until you can dye with them and they'll give you lovely new colors. You'll find the house is full of things to dye and make into something new: leftover knitting wool and fabric remnants; old sheets, bedcovers, napkins, tablecloths and other linens; unwanted outfits and sweaters. I also use old kimonos. When you start to see the possibilities of combining old fabrics and yarns you're on your way to success. Those items you can't bring yourself to throw away—beautiful lace or embroidery, fabrics with unusual textures or designs—you can recycle and make into beautiful handmade accessories.

Motifs from handmade materials

Healthy vegetables grown in a planter

The computer's convenient—but sometimes maddening!

Early morning tea with fresh-picked herbs

I try putting a fabric remnant and some yarn in a mug and popping it in the microwave. It's fun using different teas with different mordants to get color variations, and I use this technique a lot. New fabric takes on a quieter, more antique look.

After a nice cup of tea...
How about using a mug of tea for dyeing?

It's so easy to make tea in a mug and dye some small item you have at home. Without using any mordant, black tea gives a natural wheat color. It's fun spending time dyeing in the kitchen, and tea has such a soothing aroma. It makes a delicious drink, but there are other ways you can use it, too!

How to Dye with Black Tea

Tiny Heart-Shaped Sachets
(Instructions for making the sachets are on p. 72.)

Years ago, when dyes were hard to come by, housewives in Ireland had the idea of using the tea they drank every day for dyeing household linens and clothing fabrics before making them up into something new. This novel idea, and the color shades it produced, became popular all over Europe. It's an easy and convenient way to give new fabric an "antique" look.

You Will Need (for one sachet)

Fabric remnant (linen 100%)
.... 20 x 10 cm/8 x 4 in
Lace trim (cotton 100%)
.... 1 x 12 cm/0.5 x 4.75 in
No. 25 embroidery thread, white
.... approx. 50 cm/20 in

For dyeing:
Teabag .... 1 x 2 g/0.1 oz
Hot water.................. approx. 200 ml/7 fl oz
Salt..pinch

Equipment:
Mug or large cup, chopsticks or tongs, microwave oven

In Step 2, if you heat the tea in the microwave instead of using hot water, remove any metal staples in the teabag.

1 Soak fabric, lace and thread in cold water.

2 Place teabag in mug, pour in hot water and leave to cool.

3 Remove teabag, add salt to the tea and stir till dissolved. Then add the fabric, lace and thread, ensuring they are thoroughly soaked in the tea.

4 With the fabric, lace and thread totally immersed in the tea, microwave for 1 minute at 500 watts.

5 Take out the mug, stir the contents gently to prevent the dye streaking and microwave again for 30 seconds.

6 Again remove the mug, stir the contents and microwave for a further 30 seconds.

7 Allow to cool, stirring occasionally.

8 Rinse thoroughly in cold running water and dry in the fresh air, out of the sun.

9 When completely dry, press and make up the sachet.

Preparing Equipment

Dyeing in the kitchen is like cooking in the kitchen. With edible ingredients such as vegetables and teas, the usual equipment found in the kitchen can be used.

Equipment you will definitely need:

A pan or bowl

Use a pan that's big enough to allow the fabrics to move freely in the solution. Ideally the pan should be stainless steel or enamel. As long as the pan can be used on the hob and has no rust on it, it doesn't matter how old it is. Aluminum pans can be used but they are easily stained and need more cleaning.

PET drink bottle = 1 liter

1 measuring jug = 1 liter

1 teaspoon = 2.5 ml

Spoon etc. for measuring

Quantities of liquids and mordant have to be measured. (In this book I use a teaspoon of 2.5 ml for measuring small quantities of mordants.)

1 teaspoon = 2.5 g/0.1 oz of liquid and 1 g/0.04 oz of granules/powder. For convenience, use a measuring jug or PET drink bottle as a handy measure for 1 liter/2 pints.

Weighing scale

Fabrics for dyeing and materials used to make dyeing solutions have to be weighed. Ideally the scale should be in units of 1 g or 0.01 oz.

Mesh bag

• If vegetables are simmered inside a bag, they are easy to remove and discard, and the dyeing solution does not need to be strained.

• Fillable teabags or small muslin bags, mesh bags for sink garbage disposal, old stockings or old laundry net bags can be used. Choose what is suitable according to the quantity to be simmered.

• The mesh of the bag should be very fine, and non-woven bags are preferable. The bag can be closed with a rubber band.

• If some of the contents escape from the bag, the dyeing solution can be strained through a strainer lined with kitchen paper.

Chopsticks or tongs

These are useful for stirring the pan or taking things out. Large pieces of fabric become heavy and need assured handling. Wooden chopsticks will become stained and should be reserved for dyeing purposes only.

Rubber gloves

Hands may become stained, and in some cases hot liquids are used, so thick rubber gloves are recommended.

Fabrics and Other Items for Dyeing

Besides fabrics, natural materials such as wood, paper, leather and shells can be dyed. The same tea used for dyeing will produce different results depending on the material. It's a good idea to learn the characteristics of different materials.

During the dyeing process the color may look very intense, but after the fabric dries it will have only half that intensity. The color is not stable immediately after dyeing. It stabilizes after some time, when the fabric is completely dry, and only then can the final color be appreciated. Dyed colors gradually alter. Bright yellows lose their brassy look and become softer. Grays with purple or pink tones will lose those tones. This varies with different fabrics, but the color will slowly "die". The gentle "earth colors" appear a lot in this book, and these are more restrained and are very easy to live with. It's always good to remember that none of these dyes is chemical, and their colors are entirely natural.

• Materials that can be dyed

Silk ★★★★★

An animal fiber, silk is the best material for dyeing. It absorbs color at the relatively low temperature of hot bathwater.

Wool ★★★★

Also an animal fiber, wool dyes well. But the dyeing solution and mordant must be brought to the boil for the color to be absorbed. For wool it's better to add the mordant while dyeing. Wool felts very easily so use warm rather then cold water and do not wring.

Cotton; linen ★★★

Vegetable fibers can be dyed quite successfully. New fabric often has starch in it, so before dyeing it should either be soaked in hot water for 30 minutes and rinsed thoroughly, or washed in a washing machine.

Nylon; rayon ★★★

Of the synthetic fibers, nylon and rayon can be dyed as easily as cotton or linen.

Mixed synthetics ★

If dyeing wool, cotton or linen materials that contain polyester, acrylic or acetate, even in small quantity, the resulting color will be much paler. Soya milk or dairy milk can be used to improve results. See p. 37

Other materials ★★★

Other natural materials such as basket weave, terracotta, wood, washi, paper, shell buttons, plastic buttons. Choose a basket material that will not soften in the dyeing process.

• Materials that cannot be dyed

Synthetic fibers

Polyester, acrylic, acetate, plastic and coated fibers cannot be dyed.

For wool, please note the following:
• Use warm water to soak wool before dyeing.

• After bringing the dyeing solution to the boil, allow it to cool first, then add the mordant, stir and put in the wool.

• After bringing to the boil, simmer over low heat.

• Leave wool in soak until it's cool, and then rinse by adding water at the same temperature.

• Rinse gently without rubbing.

• Squeeze out excess water and spin at low speed.

Using Mordant

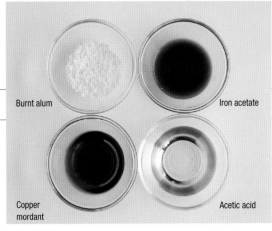

Burnt alum

Iron acetate

Copper mordant

Acetic acid

Fixing a dye with a mordant produces the final color and ensures it becomes fast. Only after the dye reacts with the mordant do you get the final color.

For these mordants or fixatives we use substances easy to obtain and drawn from alum, iron, copper and vinegar. They are all non-toxic, and are used in minute quantities and then diluted further with water, so they may be washed down the sink without problem. They can all be bought at suppliers of dyeing materials.

Note: For the same weight in grams or onnces, the quantity in tea spoons of each mordant will be different. As all weights are approximate, slight variations in quantities will not affect the final result.

Burnt alum

It produces clear yellow shades. It's used in small quantities dissolved in hot water.

Iron acetate

It gives quiet shades of gray, khaki and brown.

Copper mordant (liquid)

It gives bright shades of green, yellow and brown. It is known by various names. Ensure that the product you buy can be used in pans normally used for cooking.

Acetic acid

It gives bright color shades. I recommend 80% concentrate is effective in very small quantities. Lower concentrations are widely available, and if using them, a larger quantity will be required than stated to produce the same color effect.

Preparations for Dyeing

If materials are properly prepared for dyeing, the color will take evenly, without streaking. Follow these preparations to ensure that the dyeing solution reaches all parts of the materials evenly

• Wash well

Wool: Soak thoroughly in warm water and spin lightly before dyeing. If the fabric is soiled or contains oil or fat, leave to soak for 20 minutes in warm water containing a neutral/mild detergent, then rinse in warm water. Avoid hand rubbing or wringing. Linen; cotton: If the fabric contains starch, machine wash to remove it before dyeing. Others: Soiled fabrics should be washed in a mild detergent.

• Prepare for dyeing

To help the dyeing solution penetrate the materials evenly, knitting yarn should be wound into skeins and secured in several places with separate thread to stop it coming unwound. Tie in the ends of the yarn.

Bind the skein loosely in 4~5 places

Adapt the size of the skein to the quantity of yarn and the size of the pan.

• Weigh the materials

Weigh the fabric and yarn while dry. The quantities of dyeing solution and mordant used will depend on this weight.

• Wet the materials

Whatever materials are to be used, they should be soaked in warm water beforehand, so that they are wet when they are dyed. If dry materials are added to dyeing solution there is more likelihood of streaking.

Aftercare: Washing and Storing

• Color running

This occurs because excess color is not properly rinsed out after dyeing. Make sure the materials are rinsed thoroughly.

• Fading

Natural colors tend to fade gradually through exposure to sunlight and laundering. The earth colors selected for dyeing in this book are restrained and tend to fade less after washing.

• Laundry

Do not use bleach. Use a mild laundry detergent or other neutral detergent such as shampoo, and in principle hand-wash. Dry in a well-ventilated, shaded location.

• Pressing

The color is unstable in fabrics that have just been dyed. After some time has passed and they are completely dry, the color stabilizes and becomes the final dyed color. Forcing damp fabrics dry by ironing them may result in a color alteration and is better avoided. When pressing, avoid starting with a very hot iron. Begin with a warm iron and check on the fabric as you raise the temperature.

Let's Dye with Onions!

Onions are used in so many different dishes—they're a must in any kitchen. They are known for their cleansing effect on the blood, but the dried onion skins, too, have special powers. Don't throw them away, because they make a wonderful dye!

1	**2**
3	**4**

How to Use Onion Skins for Dyeing

The method is very simple. Use a large pan and simmer the onion skins, then add a little mordant, put in your fabric and simmer some more. That's it! Start making use of those onion skins instead of simply throwing them away!

You Will Need…

Small, undyed cloth bag (cotton 100%)
.... 30 g/1 oz

For dyeing:
Dried brown skins from about 7 onions
.... 6 g/0.2 oz
Burnt alum
.... 1.5 teaspoons (approx. 1.5 g/0.05 oz)

Equipment:
Pan (3.5-liter/4-qt), chopsticks or tongs, non-woven mesh bag, rubber band, rubber gloves

Quantities Guide
Proportional to weight of materials to be dyed:

Onion skins	Water
20%	50 times

Mordant (burnt alum)
Dissolved in a little hot water

For cotton or linen....................................5%
For silk or wool 3%

Color differences derived from different mordants:

	Burnt alum	Iron acetate	Copper mordant
Cotton			
Silk			
Wool			

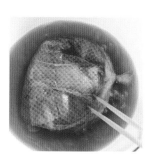

1 Preparation

• Weigh the fabric for dyeing.

• Calculate the weight of dyestuff and mordant.

• Calculate the volume of water needed. (About 50 times the weight of the fabric. The fabric should move easily in the pan.)

• Prepare the mordant. In this case we use one and a half teaspoons of burnt alum (approx. 1.5 g/0.05 oz).

• Wet the bag in water. If fabric is new, wash out any starch in advance. (For wool or silk, use warm water.)

2 Making the Dyeing Solution

• Place onion skins in a non-woven mesh bag and close the end with a rubber band, leaving plenty of room to move inside.

• Place bag of onion skins with 1 liter/2 pints of water in a pan and heat. When it comes to the boil, turn down heat and simmer for 10 minutes, then turn off heat and allow to cool.

• When cool, take out the onion skins and make up the dyeing solution by adding enough water to allow the fabric bag to move freely. In this case, 50 times the weight of the fabric bag comes to 1.5 liters/3 pints of water.

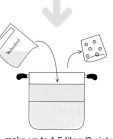

simmer for 10 minutes

make up to 1.5 liters/3 pints

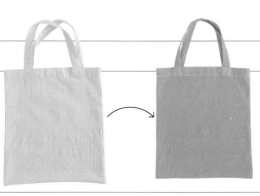

The wonder of onion skins! This natural cotton bag can be turned bright orange.

3 Dyeing and Fixing

• When the dyeing solution has completely cooled, add the mordant (burnt alum) and mix thoroughly. (Burnt alum should be dissolved first in a little hot water)

• Put on rubber gloves, place the wet fabric bag in the pan, and squeeze it to drive the dyeing solution through the fabric.

• Return over a medium heat, bring to the boil, then turn the heat down low and simmer for 10 minutes. To ensure the fabric is dyed evenly, use chopsticks or tongs to move it about in the pan from time to time.

• Turn off heat and allow to cool. Stir occasionally to ensure even dyeing. Cooling will take at least 30 minutes. If possible leave for one hour.

4 Rinsing and Drying

Once the temperature falls below 30°C, add running water to rinse. Start with warm water of about the same temperature and gradually lower the temperature until the water is running cold. Rinse well so that the water passes through the fabric. Spin lightly and dry in the fresh air, out of the sun.

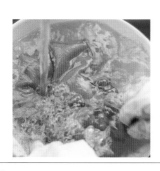

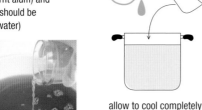

allow to cool completely

simmer for 10 minutes

allow to cool

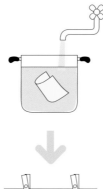

How to Dye Different Colors with the Same Dyeing Solution

Items can be dyed 3 different colors using the same basic dyeing solution. Prepare enough dyeing solution so that 3 pieces of fabric can be moved about freely, based on the guideline that it should be 50 times the weight of the fabric.

1 Preparing Materials

2 Making the Dyeing Solution

3 Dying the Fabric

When the dyeing solution has cooled, put in the 3 wet pieces of fabric and stir well. Bring to the boil over a medium heat and then simmer on a low heat for 10 minutes. Stir with chopsticks or tongs from time to time to prevent the dye streaking. Turn off the heat and allow to cool for one hour.

4 Rinsing

Remove the fabric pieces from the pan and rinse lightly in cold water. Squeeze out excess water.

5 Fixing to Create 3 Colors

Put water in 3 pans or bowls, add a different mordant to each, put 1 piece of fabric in each, and leave to soak for 30 minutes. (If the fabric is wool, bring the pan to the boil, then turn off heat and allow to cool.)

Burnt alum	Iron acetate	Copper mordant

For 1 liter of water add 1 teaspoon of burnt alum (about 1 g/0.05 oz) dissolved in hot water.	For 1 liter of water add half a teaspoon (about 1 g/0.05 oz) of iron acetate.	For 1 liter of water add a scant teaspoon (about 2 g/0.1 oz) of copper mordant.

6 Rinsing and Drying

1 teaspoon = 2.5 ml

Mini Raffia Baskets

(Instructions for making the baskets are on p. 73.)

The skins of onions have been used since ancient times as an excellent dye source. By using different mordants and varying the quantities used, you can obtain a wide range of shades. Coordinate colors to make yourself a little basket that is truly original!

You Will Need...

Natural raffia .. 14 strands (about 16 g/0.5 oz)

For dyeing:
Onion skins................................. 8 g/0.25 oz
Burnt alum.....1 teaspoon (about 1 g/0.05 oz)
Iron acetate .... scant 1/2 teaspoon
(about 1 g/0.05 oz)

Equipment:
Pan (3.5-liter/4-qt), 2 bowls (1.5-liter/3-pint), non-woven mesh bag, rubber band, chopsticks or tongs, rubber gloves

1 Preparation

Prepare the materials and equipment. Wash the raffia and leave in water to soak.

2 Making the Dyeing Solution

Place mesh bag containing onion skins in pan with 1 liter/2 pints of water, bring to the boil over medium heat, turn down heat and simmer for 10 minutes. When cool, remove onion skins and make up the dyeing solution to 1.5 liters/3 pints.

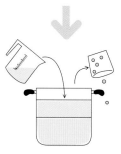

simmer for 10 minutes

make up to 1.5 liters/3 pints

3 Dyeing the Raffia

Put soaked raffia into the dyeing solution, and place over a medium heat. When it boils turn down heat and simmer for 10 minutes. Leave to cool, stirring occasionally

simmer for 10 minutes

4 Fixing

Make 2 types of mordant by putting 700 ml/1.5 pints of water in each of 2 bowls. To one, add 1 teaspoon (about 1 g/0.05 oz) of burnt alum dissolved in a little hot water and stir. In the other dissolve a scant half teaspoon (about 1 g/0.05 oz) of iron acetate. Add 7 strands of the dyed raffia to each and soak.

• Burnt alum gives an orange shade

soak for 30 minutes

• Iron acetate gives a dark brown shade

soak for 30 minutes

5 Rinsing and Drying

Rinse well in running water, squeeze out excess water, and dry in fresh air, out of the sun.

6 Making the Basket

Use the 3 colors of raffia: 1 undyed and 2 dyed, to make a basket. See p. 73 for instructions.

Mosaic-Patterned Plant Pots

You Will Need...

Small, unglazed plant pot...........................1
Egg shells..............................from 3~4 eggs

For dyeing:
Onion skins................................. 4 g/0.15 oz
Burnt alum.....1 teaspoon (about 1 g/0.05 oz)

Equipment:
Pan (2-liter/2-qt), non-woven mesh bag,
rubber band, chopsticks or tongs, rubber
gloves

1 Preparation

Place onion skins in mesh bag and close end
with a rubber band. Wash egg shells
thoroughly and leave to soak in warm water.

2 Making the Dyeing Solution

Place bag of onion skins in pan with 800
ml/1.75 pints of water, bring to the boil,
simmer for 5 minutes and turn off heat.
When cool, remove onion skins and make up
the dyeing solution to 1 liter/2 pints.

simmer for 5 minutes

3 Fixing the Dye

Add burnt alum dissolved in a little hot water
to the dyeing solution and put in half the egg
shells. Bring to the boil, simmer for two
minutes and turn off heat. Add the rest of the
egg shells and leave to soak for 5 minutes.

soak for 5 minutes

4 Rinsing and Drying

After 5 minutes take out egg shells, rinse
well and leave to dry in a shady location.

5 Applying the Egg Shells

When the egg shells are completely dry, use
adhesive to stick pieces onto the plant pot to
make a mosaic design.

Cushions

You Will Need...

Undyed cushion cover (100% linen)
.....35 cm/13.75 in square (about 100 g/3.5 oz)
Tyrolean ribbon.........................as necessary

For dyeing:
Onion skins................................. 12 g/0.4 oz
Iron acetate ...2 teaspoons (about 2 g/0.1 oz)

Equipment:
Large pan (8-liter/8-qt), non-woven mesh
bag, rubber band, chopsticks or tongs,
rubber gloves

Dyeing Procedure:

❶ Leave cushion cover and ribbons to soak
in water.

❷ Place bag of onion skins in pan with
2 liters/4 pints of water, bring to the boil,
and simmer for 10 minutes. Add water to
make up dyeing solution to 4 liters/4 qts.

❸ Add 2 teaspoons (about 2 g/0.1 oz) of
iron acetate, add cushion cover, bring to
the boil and simmer for 5 minutes.

❹ Add ribbon, turn off heat, and leave to
soak until cool.

❺ When cool, rinse thoroughly in cold water
and dry in the fresh air, out of the sun.

❻ Decorate the cushion cover with the
ribbon.

simmer for 10 minutes

simmer for 5 minutes

Drawstring Bag

You Will Need...

Undyed drawstring bag (100% cotton or linen)
about 20 x 13 cm/8 x 5 in
...................................1 (about 20 g/0.75 oz)

For dyeing:
Onion skins................................. 3 g/0.1 oz
Burnt alum.....1 teaspoon (about 1 g/0.05 oz)

Equipment:
Pan (2.5-liter/3-qt), non-woven mesh bag,
rubber band, chopsticks or tongs, rubber
gloves

Dyeing Procedure:

❶ Make 1 liter/2 pints of dyeing solution.

❷ Use the same quantity of dyeing solution
as for the raffia bags on p. 14, and add
burnt alum or iron acetate.

❸ Add drawstring bag, bring to the boil, and
simmer for 5~10 minutes.

❹ When cool, rinse thoroughly in cold water
and dry in the fresh air, out of the sun.

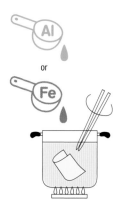

simmer for 5~10 minutes

1 teaspoon = 2.5 ml

Color Palette

Vegetables, teas and other natural ingredients can be used for kitchen dyeing, and the same tea may give different shades depending on other conditions. I once used new green tea and older green tea for dyeing and got entirely different colors! Water and heat are involved in the dyeing process, and even when dyeing under exactly the same conditions subtle differences will emerge, so it's difficult to dye to exactly the same shade. But when you think that the shade you've produced is totally unique it comes to feel very special. And you have the fun of wondering what you'll get next time, sometimes obtaining totally unexpected shades! Sample nature's colors with an open mind!

Red and pink shades

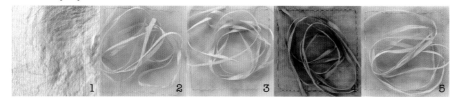

1 Purple perilla
2 Rose
3 Hibiscus
4 Raspberry
5 Black soybean
6 Blackberry
7 Cherry sage
8 Red wine
9 Marigold

Blue and purple shades

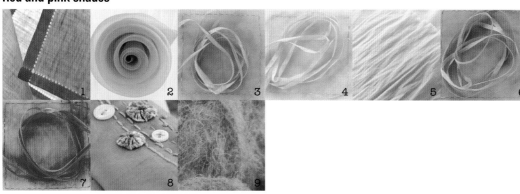

1 Black grapes
2 Blueberry
3 Blue mallow
4 Meadow sage
5 Lavender

Gray shades

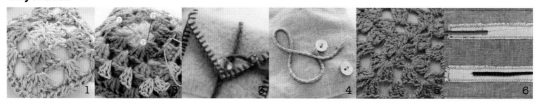

1 Hibiscus tea
2 Hibiscus tea
3 Black soybean
4 Lavender
5 Earl Grey tea
6 Sweet chestnut

Beige shades

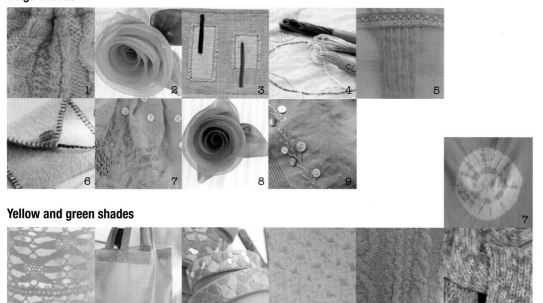

1 Mandarin orange
2 Rose
3 Sweet chestnut
4 Spices
5 Apple tea
6 Black soybean
7 Oolong tea
8 Rose
9 Onion

Yellow and green shades

1 Gardenia
2 Onion
3 Onion
4 Chamomile tea
5 Mandarin orange
6 Marigold
7 Turmeric

SPRING

Kitchen Dyeing for Spring

In spring I want to drink tea that reminds me it's spring! But when I open my cupboards, what do I find inside? Lots of teas I've forgotten about! So I make space and use all the old tea for dyeing. I also find spices well past their use-by dates. Do I throw them away? Of course not. I think about dyeing something!

These crocheted squares can be any size I want. By adding two more rows to the coaster size, I make a teapot mat.

Chamomile Tea

Chamomile tea with its sweet, apple-like fragrance is a herb tea known for promoting restful sleep. You make it by pouring hot water over chamomile, leaving it for three minutes, and adding warm milk. This is the tea Peter Rabbit was given when he caught cold. Used for dyeing, it produces the soft shades typical of herbs.

	Burnt alum	Iron acetate	Copper mordant
Cotton			
Silk			
Wool			

You Will Need…

Crocheted squares (100% cotton)
...................................3 (approx. 15 g/0.5 oz)

For dyeing:
Chamomile teabags
.... about 5 (approx. 10 g/0.35 oz)
Burnt alum.....1 teaspoon (about 1 g/0.05 oz)

Equipment:
Pan (2.5-liter/3-qt), chopsticks or tongs, rubber gloves

Quantities Guide
Proportional to weight of materials to be dyed:

Chamomile tea	Water
60%	60 times

Mordant (burnt alum)
Dissolved in a little hot water

For cotton or linen....................................6%
For silk or wool 4%

Change the mordant to change the shade

When fixing the dye (Step 4), using iron acetate or copper mordant instead of alum gives different shades.

Add a scant 1/2 teaspoon (about 1 g/0.05 oz) of iron acetate to 1 liter/2 pints of water, to get a light brown.

Add 1 teaspoon (about 2.5 g/0.1 oz) of copper mordant to 1 liter/2 pints of water, to get a mustard yellow.

1 Preparation

Crochet the squares (see p. 66). Prepare the materials and equipment. Soak the squares thoroughly with warm water, rinse and spin lightly.

2 Making the Dyeing Solution

Place the chamomile teabags and 700 ml/1.5 pints of water in a pan, bring to the boil over a medium heat, then turn down heat and simmer for 10 minutes. When cool, take out the teabags and make up the dyeing solution to 1 liter/2 pints.

simmer for 10 minutes

make up to 1 liter/2 pints

3 Dyeing the Squares

Put the wet squares in the dyeing solution, bring to the boil over a medium heat, turn down the heat and simmer for 10 minutes. Leave to cool, stirring occasionally.

soak for 30 minutes

stir occasionally to prevent streaks

4 Fixing the Dye

Make the mordant by adding one teaspoon (about 1 gm/0.05 oz) of burnt alum dissolved in a little hot water in a bowl containing 1 liter/2 pints of water and stir. When the squares are cool, rinse them, place them in the mordant and leave to soak for 30 minutes.

leave to soak for 30 minutes

If using squares crocheted from wool, add the mordant at Step 3, stir and simmer.

5 Rinsing and Drying

Rinse well in running water, spin lightly, and dry in the fresh air, out of the sun.

1 teaspoon = 2.5 ml

I had some leftover yarns of wool, silk, and cotton that I had dyed little by little. I crocheted squares and used them to make small handy accessories. It's fascinating to see how different yarns take on different shades even when dyed in the same solution. The quantities are small so a small pan is big enough.

Hibiscus Tea

Small Sewing Accessories
(Instructions for making these items are on p. 67.)

See p. 57 for dyeing instructions.

Hibiscus tea is very popular for its beauty benefits. Many people drinking this lovely ruby-red tea must think what a good dye it should make. Here I've used a simmering dyeing method to get slightly different shades. The red gives way to beige and gray.

Using the patterned fabric of an old kimono and some old silk, I made a pair of mini-sized drawstring bags. The bases are made of knitted silk, the top parts are sewn separately, and then the two are hand-stitched together.

Green Tea

Knitted Silk Drawstring Bags
(Instructions for making these bags are on p. 70.)

See p. 56 for dyeing instructions.

Black tea is made by fermenting tea leaves, while for green tea the leaves are fired but do not ferment. It's astonishing that the same leaves produce such different tasting teas. This is also true of how they dye. Different types of green tea give slightly different shades. Of course, *matcha* can also be used.

A square of fabric made special using pepper

Embroidery threads dyed in three shades with cloves

I dyed a well-used linen cloth with pepper, and skeins of white embroidery thread into three different shades with wonderfully aromatic cloves. I decorated the cloth with spots and circles to give texture, using only the simplest embroidery stitches.

Pepper and Cloves

Embroidered Cloth Wrapper
(Instructions for making the wrapper are on p. 74.)

See p. 58 for dyeing instructions.

At home I cook largely Japanese food and I don't use spices very often so they sit on the shelf with nothing to do. When used for dyeing white and black pepper give gentle shades, however much you use. Cloves look like stubby nails. They have a long history as an aromatic dyeing substance.

It's fun to use different mordants to give different color tones

I used cinnamon to dye a new wicker basket to make it look well-used, and then kept small sewing items in it. It looks homely with the lovely old fabrics in it. Besides wicker, you can use willow, straw or bamboo.

Cinnamon

See p. 58 for dyeing instructions.

Cinnamon is a must for flavoring apple pie. To use it as a dye, the powder can be dissolved and the sticks can be chopped up very finely. With burnt alum as a mordant you get a pinkish beige. With iron-based mordant you get the color of milky cocoa. What's special is the lingering hint of its aroma.

Fit the glass holder in place and then tighten the thread at the bottom.

I use gardenia seeds every year to color the traditional chestnut puree I make for our New Year celebrations. With the leftover seeds I dyed cotton torchon lace and used it to turn a kitchen cloth into a tablecloth. When dyeing the lace I added white embroidery thread so that I wouldn't have to buy some and try and match up the color.

Gardenia Seeds

Lace-Trimmed Tablecloth and Glass Holders
(Instructions for making the items are on p. 81.)

See p. 59 for dyeing instructions.

Heavily-scented gardenia flowers have long been used for perfumes. The seeds have commercial value as a coloring agent for Japanese confectionery and candy, and in our house I use them when I boil chestnuts or sweet potatoes. Dyeing with them always gives yellow, whatever mordant I use, and I'm surprised how bright it is.

SUMMER

Kitchen Dyeing for Summer

Bright yellows that reflect the strong summer sun. Earthy pastels with their gentle shades. The pinks and purples of well-loved flowers and fruits.

Dyeing with flower petals is simple and uses acetic acid, so it's different from the basic dyeing method. Try it out when you want to have fun with colors. I also recommend tie-dyeing when you're in a playful mood. Either way, these are processes you can enjoy with children, so they're ideal summer vacation projects. Let's savor the special delights of summer dyeing!

To get a unique and individual design, cover parts of the fabric with cling film and secure it tightly with rubber bands, or try other ways of preventing the dye from reaching certain areas. How will the pattern turn out? The moments before you remove the rubber bands are tense with expectation...

Turmeric

Turmeric is sometimes called Indian saffron because it's used to give curries their yellow color. It has no spicy smell or taste. It's known as a general colorant for foodstuffs and as a health food, and like ginger it's the root of the plant that is used. It's sold powdered or sliced.

	Burnt alum	Iron acetate	Copper mordant
Cotton			
Silk			
Wool	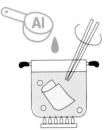		

You Will Need...

Pale blue T-shirt for 4~5 year old
(100% cotton)............1 (approx. 80 g/2.8 oz)
White buttons for decoration

For dyeing:
Turmeric powder.........................20 g/0.7 oz
Burnt alum...4 teaspoons (about 4 g/0.15 oz)

Equipment:
Pan (5-liter/6-qt), chopsticks or tongs, rubber bands, cling film, egg whisk, cooking paper, strainer, rubber gloves

Quantities Guide
Proportional to weight of materials to be dyed:

Turmeric	Water
25%	40 times

Mordant (burnt alum)
Dissolved in a little hot water

For cotton or linen....................................5%
For silk or wool 3%

Tips

- Use a large pan to give the garment plenty of space and prevent streaks. For dyeing adult-sized garments, try small ones first, such as tank tops.
- Pink and red T-shirts can also be dyed with turmeric to create pretty colors.

1 Preparation

Draw your tie-dyeing design on the T-shirt.
For the areas where you want to block out the dye, gather the fabric together on the outside of the T-shirt, and tie it up tightly with rubber bands. Cover with cling film and secure the cling film tightly with rubber bands.

Place buttons under the fabric and cover with cling film to get polka dots.

Soak the T-shirt and buttons for decoration in warm water.

Soak the T-shirt and buttons for decoration in warm water.

2 Making the Dyeing Solution

Dissolve the turmeric in a little hot water, add to 1.5 liters/3 pints of water in a pan and bring to the boil over a medium heat. Turn off heat and allow to cool. Line the inside of a strainer with cooking paper, and carefully strain the dyeing solution. Then add water to make it up to 3.2 liters/6.75 pints.

dissolve thoroughly using an egg whisk

strain carefully to remove lumps

3 Dyeing and Fixing

Add burnt alum to the dyeing solution, then put in the wet T-shirt and buttons and bring to the boil over a medium heat. Turn down the heat and simmer for 10 minutes. Leave to cool, stirring occasionally.

simmer for 10 minutes

Stir occasionally while it is cooling to prevent streaks.

4 Rinsing and Drying

Rinse quickly, remove the rubber bands and then rinse thoroughly. Spin lightly and dry in the fresh air, out of the sun.

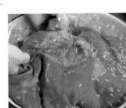

5 Adding Buttons

Finally, sew on dyed buttons as desired to highlight the design.

I tried dyeing with some lavender potpourri. As I heated it the whole house filled with the fragrance of lavender. And it worked! I used all my linen remnants and made soap bags.

Lavender

Popular lavender is seen as pure and clean and is widely used in cosmetics, toiletries and perfumes for the soothing effect of its fragrance. Many people assume it can be used as a dye to obtain its delicate lavender color, but regardless of whether you use flowers, leaves or stems, dyeing by simmering gives you a soft earth shade.

You Will Need...

Fabric remnants (100% linen)
.... 2 (approx. 20 g/0.7 oz)

For dyeing:
Dried lavender flowers............... 20 g/0.7 oz
Iron acetate
.........Scant 1/2 teaspoon (about 1 g/0.05 oz)

Equipment:
Pan (2-liter/2-qt), mesh bag, rubber band, chopsticks or tongs, rubber gloves

Quantities Guide
Proportional to weight of materials to be dyed:

Dried lavender flowers	Water
50%	50 times

Mordant (iron acetate)	
	Dissolved in a little hot water

For cotton or linen....................................5%
For silk or wool 3%

Tips

- Using fresh instead of dried lavender, for silk or wool remnants use the same weight of lavender as fabric, and for cotton or linen use 150~200% of the weight of the fabric. Chop the lavender finely just before using it.

1 Preparation

Soak the linen remnants in warm water, and when completely wet squeeze out excess water.
(For new fabric, soak in hot water for 20 minutes, and rinse.)

2 Making the Dyeing Solution

Place the lavender in a mesh bag and close with a rubber band.

Place in a pan with 800 ml/1.75 pints of water, bring to the boil over a medium heat, then turn down heat and simmer for 10 minutes. Turn off heat and allow to cool. When cool, remove the lavender and make up the dyeing solution to 1 liter/2 pints.

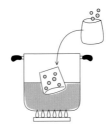

simmer for 10 minutes

make up to 1 liter/2 pints

3 Dyeing and Fixing

- When completely cool, add iron acetate to the dyeing solution and stir well.
- Put in the fabric and stir until fabric absorbs dyeing solution. Bring to the boil over a medium heat, then simmer for 10 minutes over a low heat.
- Turn off heat, and leave to cool, stirring occasionally.
- If dyeing torchon lace, remove it just before the pan comes to the boil.

simmer for 10 minutes

4 Rinsing and Drying

Rinse well in running water until the water runs clear, spin lightly and dry in the fresh air, out of the sun.

5 Making the Soap Bag

The color is not completely fixed while the fabric is wet, so allow to dry completely before pressing with a warm iron.
See p. 75 for further instructions.

1 teaspoon = 2.5 ml

Burnt alum

Copper mordant

Iron acetate

I was thrilled to be given a large bouquet of roses and for days enjoyed their wonderful color and scent. Then I tried using the stems and leaves of three roses to dye with. Silk organdie is very fine and light and dyes well with very little solution.

Fresh Rose

More and more people are growing roses for their elegant flowers and beguiling scent. The stems and leaves can be used for dyeing regardless of the color of the blooms, so don't throw away the cuttings after you prune your roses but try dyeing with them. Try it, too, if you receive roses as a gift.

You Will Need...(for 2 corsages)

Bias-cut organdie (100% silk)
For flower heads
2 x 12 x 80~100 cm/4.75 x 31.5~39.5 in
For leaves and stems
2 x 14 x 25 cm/5.5 x 9.75 in
.... total weight 8 g/0.25 oz

For dyeing:
Rose stems and leaves .... 30 g/1 oz
Burnt alum (for flower heads)
.....................1 teaspoon (about 1 g/0.05 oz)
Iron acetate (for leaves and base)
.... 1/4 teaspoon (about 0.6 g/0.02 oz)

Equipment:
Pan (3-liter/3-qt), small pan (1-liter/2-pint), kitchen scissors, mesh bag, rubber bands, chopsticks or tongs, rubber gloves

Quantities Guide
Proportional to weight of materials to be dyed:

Rose stems and leaves	Water
4 times	200 times

Change the mordant to change the color shade

Copper mordant was used as the mordant for the rose in the lower corsage in the photo p. 30.
Copper mordant
.... scant 1 teaspoon (about 2g/0.1 oz)
Add mordant to dyeing solution for flower heads. Dyeing procedure is the same as for burnt alum.

Tips

- Organdie is light but takes up surprising space, so decide on the quantity of water after immersing the organdie in it. Then decide the quantity of mordant from the volume of water.

- See p. 76 for guidance on mordant quantity when using fabrics other than organdie.

1 Preparation

Soak the organdie in warm water, and squeeze out excess water without stretching fabric.
Cut up the rose stems and leaves very finely, place in a mesh bag and close it with a rubber band.

2 Making the Dyeing Solution

Place the rose and 1 liter/2 pints of water in the pan, and bring to the boil over a medium heat. Turn down heat and simmer for 15 minutes. Then turn off heat, and when cool, take out the rose and make up the dyeing solution to 1.6 liters/3.5 pints (so that the 2 pieces of fabric can move about easily).

simmer for 15 minutes

make up to 1.6 liters/3.5 pints

- Divide the dyeing solution into two, keeping 1.2 liters/2.5 pints in the large pan and putting 400 ml/0.8 pints in the small pan.

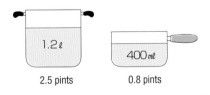

1.2 ℓ	400 ㎖
2.5 pints	0.8 pints

3 Dyeing and Fixing

Add burnt alum to the larger quantity of dyeing solution and stir well. Put in the organdie fabric for the flower heads and stir until the fabric absorbs the dyeing solution. Bring to the boil over a low heat and then turn off heat.

for flower heads

- Add iron acetate to the dyeing solution in the small pan, put in the organdie fabric for the leaves and base, bring to the boil over a low heat and turn off heat.

for leaves and base

4 Rinsing and Drying

Rinse both pieces of organdie well in running water, reshape without stretching, and dry in the fresh air out of the sun.

5 Making the Corsages

The color is not completely fixed while the fabric is wet, so dry thoroughly and then press with a warm iron. See p. 76 for further instructions.

Dyeing with Dark Red Rose Petals

Dark red rose petals can be used to give a pink dye when fixed with vinegar.
See p. 33 for dyeing instructions.

For 1 corsage of silk organdie, use 30 g/1 oz of dark red rose petals, and 800 ml /1.75 pints of water with 30 ml/0.06 pint of 80% acetic acid

1 teaspoon = 2.5 ml

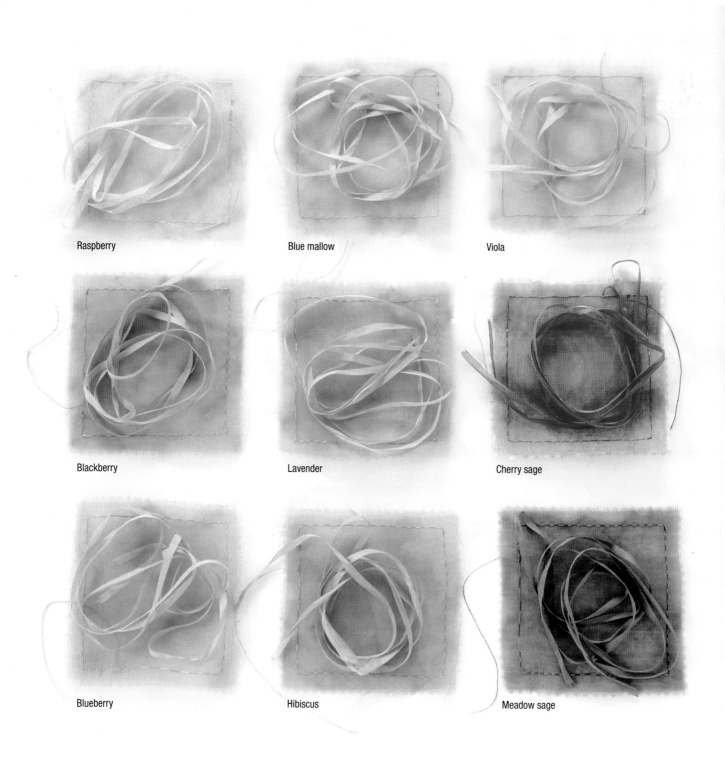

Raspberry

Blue mallow

Viola

Blackberry

Lavender

Cherry sage

Blueberry

Hibiscus

Meadow sage

These colors are produced using vinegar. Red and blue dye sources are vulnerable to heat and light and gradually fade to become more subtle shades. These colors can be enjoyed in the same way as the changing color in a garden.

Blueberry

Organdie Sachet
(Instructions for making the sachet are on p. 77.)

The natural red/purple pigment called anthocyrian contained in blueberries dyes to very pretty shades. Any fruit or flower that stains your fingers pink or purple when you pick them can be used to dye in the same way. The pigment is not affected by freezing, so frozen blueberries can be used. Fabrics in strong colors dye well.

You Will Need…(for one sachet)

Organdie sachet (100% silk)
...................................1 (approx. 2 g/0.1 oz)
Ribbon (100% silk) .... as required

For dyeing:
Frozen blueberries .... 20 g/0.7 oz
80% acetic acid.......... about 20 ml/0.04 pint

Equipment:
Pan (1.5-liter/3-pint), mesh bag (stocking), rubber band, rubber gloves

Quantities Guide
Proportional to weight of materials to be dyed:

Blueberries	Water
10 times	250 times

Mordant (80% acetic acid)

 For 500 ml/1 pint of dyeing solution

For cotton or linen.....approx. 30 ml/0.06 pint
For silk ....approx. 20 ml/0.04 pint
(Wool is not suitable because it requires high-temperature dyeing)

Tips

• Red and blue dyes don't like heat, so the dyestuff is not heated but kneaded in cold water containing acetic acid, and the fabric is left to soak in it. Silk is perfect for this because it dyes very well even at low temperatures.

• Washing with alkaline detergent may cause a change in the color. Use a mild detergent, dry in a shaded location and avoid pressing with a hot iron. When not in use wrap in tissue paper and store in a sealed polythene bag, to prevent color changes.

1 Preparation

Make the sachet following instructions on p. 77, and soak it with the ribbon in warm water.

2 Making the Dyeing Solution

Put the blueberries in a bag made of an old stocking. Add 20 ml/0.04 pint of acetic acid to 500 ml/1 pint of water in a pan. Put in the blueberries and gently knead them to a pulp to extract the dye and make a dyeing solution.

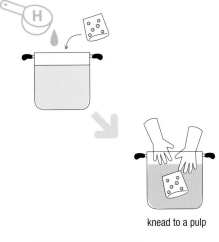

knead to a pulp

3 Dyeing and Fixing

Put the wet sachets into the dyeing solution, and leave to soak for 3 hours, occasionally stirring or working the dye through the fabric. Working the blueberry bag and sachet fabric together is more effective. If the pan is placed in a bath of hot water or warmed to about 40°C at this time, the dyed color will be stronger.

4 Rinsing and Drying

Rinse well in running water and dry in the fresh air, out of the sun.

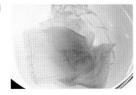

5 Making the Sachet

Fill the sachet with potpourri and tie it around with ribbon. Alternatively, sachets can be used as appliqué to add a design to a T-shirt.
For further instructions see p. 77.

 1 teaspoon = 2.5 ml

33

A fleetingly beautiful color to enjoy

I wanted to serve homemade purple perilla juice (see p. 60 for the recipe) like this to my guests, so I left some little linen napkins to soak for 24 hours in a purple perilla dye. For wool you have to use the simmering procedure, and then by using burnt alum as a mordant you get pinky beige shades, and with iron acetate you get purplish gray shades.

Purple Perilla

Small Linen Napkins

See p. 60 for dyeing instructions.

Purple perilla, sometimes called red shiso after its Japanese name, has richly colored leaves, and I gather it from the garden at the height of summer. There's more than enough to make juice for the whole summer season, so I tried using some to dye linen napkins. Unlike silk, cotton and linen do not keep the new color for long, and the red-purple fades and turns to a pinkish beige.

Autumn

Kitchen Dyeing for Autumn

The days are still warm, but when Japanese black grapes appear in our stores I know autumn is on its way. And then I spot chestnuts! It's the time of year I keep a close eye on the greengrocer. I keep the skins of black grapes and the water left from cooking chestnuts because they both make great dyes.

Health teas are good at this time of year. When I see the benefits they bring, I want to buy them all. Sipping piping hot tea always helps me unwind. I've test-dyed with all sorts of teas, wondering what colors I will get.

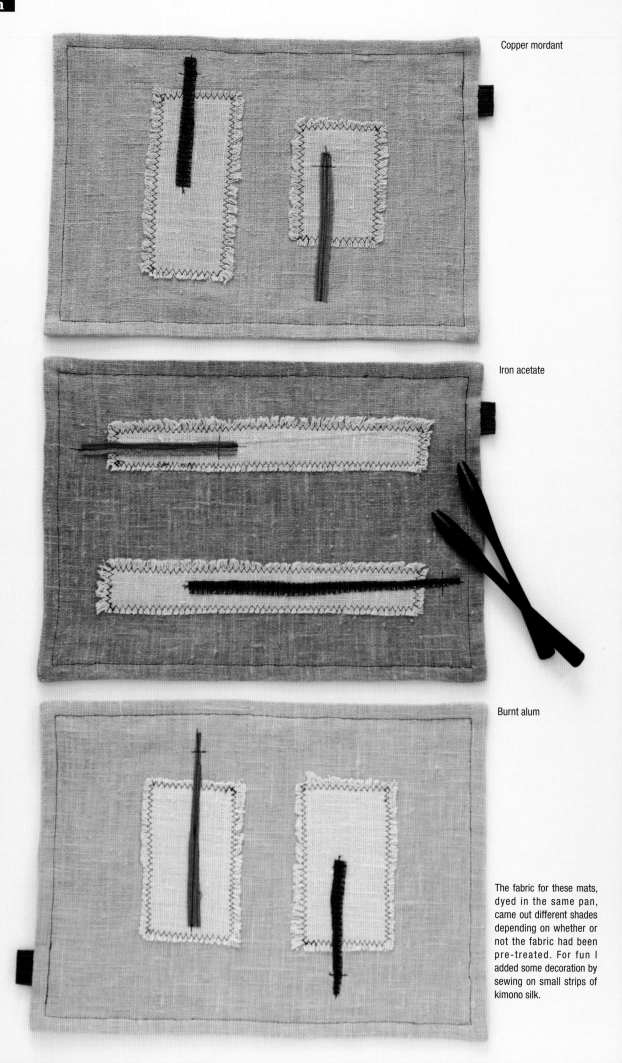

Copper mordant

Iron acetate

Burnt alum

The fabric for these mats, dyed in the same pan, came out different shades depending on whether or not the fabric had been pre-treated. For fun I added some decoration by sewing on small strips of kimono silk.

Chestnuts

I have a cooking method that produces tasty chestnuts and is good for dyeing, too. You boil the chestnuts in water until they are as soft as you want them, and then you leave them to cool in the cooking water. The chestnuts are easier to peel, and the liquid becomes a more concentrated dyeing solution. Something to remember when you next cook chestnuts to make a French dessert!

You Will Need…
(for the gray mat shown in the center)

Linen-mix fabric (65% linen, 35% cotton)
For the mat (pre-treated)
.... 2 x 22 x 30 cm/8.75 x 11.75 in
For contrasting fabric (not pre-treated)
.... 1 x 40 x 6 cm/15.75 x 2.25 in
.... Total weight approx. 50 g/1.75 oz

For dyeing:
Fresh chestnuts .... 1 kg/2.2 lb
Iron acetate
.... 1 teaspoon (approx. 2.5 g/0.1 oz)
Unprocessed soya milk .... 330 ml/11.2 fl oz

Equipment:
Pan (4-liter/5-qt), chopsticks or tongs

Quantities Guide
Proportional to weight of materials to be dyed:

Chestnuts	Water
20 times	40 times

(Weight of chestnuts is 20 times weight of material, but water left after boiling chestnuts is used for dyeing.)

Mordant (iron acetate)

For cotton or linen................................... 5%
For silk or wool 3%

Change the mordant to change the shade

- In photo p. 36, copper mordant was used for the top mat and burnt alum for the bottom mat.
  Copper mordant.................................. 10%
  Burnt alum 5%
  of weight of fabric to be dyed

1 Preparation

- Cut the fabric to the sizes required and soak it in water. If it's new and contains starch, wash it to remove the starch.

- Put the 2 pieces of fabric for the mat into 330 ml/ 11.2 fl oz of unprocessed soya milk (or dairy milk) diluted with 1 liter/2 pints of water and leave to soak for 1 hour, occasionally squeezing the liquid through the fabric. Spin the fabric lightly without rinsing it and dry swiftly in the sun.

- Immediately before dyeing, soak the mat fabric and contrasting fabric in water.

Pre-Treatment

- Cotton and linen come from vegetable sources, and enriching them with protein by soaking them in soya or dairy milk produces a stronger color when they are dyed. They become like animal-derived silk or wool, and are easier to dye.

- Pre-treating thicker fabrics such as canvas or Indian cotton, or fabrics containing polyester, makes them easier to dye and gives better results. But this is only true when fabrics are soaked in soya or dairy milk.

- Unlike dairy milk, unprocessed soya milk has no smell when dry. Treated fabric can be kept for up to a year before dyeing. The smell of dairy milk disappears after dyeing.

2 Making the Dyeing Solution

Boil 1 kg/2.2 lb of chestnuts in 1.5 liters/3 pints of water until they reach the desired softness, then turn off heat and leave to cool in the pan.
Remove the chestnuts and add water to the pan to make up the dyeing solution to 2 liters/4 pints.

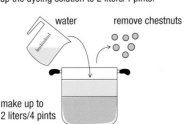

water   remove chestnuts

make up to
2 liters/4 pints

3 Dyeing and Fixing

Add iron acetate to the dyeing solution, then put in the fabrics and stir around. Bring to the boil over a medium heat, then turn down heat and simmer for 10 minutes. Leave to cool, stirring occasionally.

stir occasionally
to avoid streaks

simmer for 10 minutes

4 Rinsing and Drying

Rinse well in running water, spin lightly and dry in the fresh air, out of the sun.

5 Making the Tea Mat

See p. 78 for instructions.
There's also a recipe for making chestnut paste.

It's easy to dye silk stoles and scarves and give them a style makeover. Decorating the edges with beads or spangles adds a little extra weight and the stole will sit a little more closely to the body. You can, of course, try the same thing with cotton or linen scarves.

Black Grapes

The most popular variety of Japanese black grapes is cultivated in a region with views of Mt Fuji. Knowing their sweet, crisp flavor and blue-black skins are transferred to ice cream and sherbet, I tried dyeing with them. The skins are normally discarded and not eaten, but here they have a role all their own.

You Will Need...

Stole (100% silk) ....
35 x 130 cm/14 x 51 in (approx. 15 g/0.5 oz)

For dyeing:
Skins of black grapes
....................3 bunches (approx. 230 g/8 oz)
80% acetic acid............ approx. 30 ml/1 fl oz

Equipment:
Pan (3.5-liter/4-qt), mixer, stocking type mesh bag, rubber band, rubber gloves

Quantities Guide
Proportional to weight of materials to be dyed:

Grape skins	Warm water
150%	100 times

Mordant (80% acetic acid)

 For 1 liter/2 pints of dyeing solution

For cotton or linen......... approx. 30 ml/1 fl oz
For silk or wool .... approx. 20 ml/0.7 fl oz
(Wool cannot be dyed with this low temperature method.)

Tips

- All varieties of black grapes are suitable. Every time you eat grapes, save the skins, put them in a plastic bag and keep them in the freezer.
- Delaware grapes give the color of rose wine.
- Dyed this way, cotton and linen do not keep the color very long compared to silk.
- It's an acid-based dye and so the color will change if the item is washed with an alkaline detergent. Wash with a neutral detergent, dry in the shade, and avoid using a hot iron. When not in use store the item in a sealed polythene bag.

1 Preparation

Soak the stole.

2 Making the Dyeing Solution

Place the grape skins and 1.5 liters/3 pints of warm water in an electric mixer, and add the acetic acid. It may be necessary to divide the quantities and mix more than once.

Mix for 5 or 6 seconds.

Strain the mixture through an old stocking or fine mesh bag to obtain the dyeing solution.

3 Soaking and Dyeing

Put the dyeing solution in a pan, add the stole and leave to soak for 2 hours.

Move the stole about from time to time to prevent streaking. Chopsticks or tongs may damage the stole, so wear rubber gloves and use your hands.

Place the pan over a low heat, and warm to about 40°C. Turn off the heat and leave to soak for a further 2 hours. (For cotton or linen items more difficult to dye, repeat this procedure one more time.)

40°C

4 Rinsing and Drying

Rinse well in running water, spin lightly and dry in the fresh air, out of the sun.

gradually add water to pan

5 Decorating with Beads

See p. 79 for instructions.

🥄 1 teaspoon = 2.5 ml

I had a linen-mix stole in a natural color that I used a lot over one summer and it became very soft and pliable. So I tried dyeing it to make it look more chic. By soaking different parts in different mordants I obtained a complex mix of shades in stripes and a more fashionable look.

Persimmon Leaf Tea

Persimmon leaf tea has a fresh taste with a hint of mint, and it's good for cleaning the palette after eating greasy food. The green fruit of the persimmon (*kaki*) has been used for dyeing since ancient times, and *kakishibu* (persimmon juice) is a traditional dyeing medium in Japan. I wanted to use the tea I had for dyeing.

You Will Need...

Stole (silk/cotton mix)
.... 1 x approx. 100 g/3.5 oz

For dyeing:
Persimmon leaf tea.................. 50 g/1.75 oz
Burnt alum..... 5 teaspoons (about 5 g/0.2 oz)
Iron acetate ... 2 teaspoons (about 2 g/0.1 oz)

Equipment:
Pan (6-liter/6.5-qt), chopsticks or tongs, mesh bag, rubber band

Quantities Guide
Proportional to weight of materials to be dyed:

Persimmon leaf tea	Water

50%	35 times

Mordant (burnt alum)

 Dissolved in a little hot water

For cotton or linen.....................5%
For silk or wool 3%

Mordant (iron acetate)

For cotton or linen.....................5%
For silk or wool 3%

Tips

• For a stronger color, simmer the stole in the dyeing solution before proceeding to Step 2 and adding the burnt alum.

1 Preparation

Put the persimmon leaf tea and 2 liters/4 pints of warm water in a pan, and bring to the boil over a medium heat. Simmer over low heat for 15 minutes, then turn off heat, remove the tea and make up the dyeing solution to 3.5 liters/7 pints.
Soak the stole in water.

simmer for 15 minutes

2 Dyeing and Fixing the Base Color

Add burnt alum to the dyeing solution, put in the stole and stir in the solution, bring to the boil over a medium heat and simmer for 10 minutes. Turn off the heat and leave to cool, stirring occasionally. When cool, rinse the stole well and spin lightly.

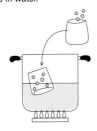

simmer for 10 minutes

leave to cool

 rinse in running water

3 Tying the Stole

To create a pattern of stripes, tie tight knots in the stole in several places. If the knots are too loose, the color difference will not be so pronounced, so tie the knots tightly.

4 Second Fixing

Add iron acetate to 3 liters/6 pints of water and dissolve to make a fixing solution. Put in the stole tied with knots and soak for 10 minutes.

The iron acetate will add a layer of gray and change the color.

 Leave the ends of the stole out of the fixing solution to retain the earlier color, for a better effect.

5 Decorating with Beads

Taking care to avoid the areas not soaked in the second fixing solution, squeeze out the liquid and rinse quickly, then undo the knots. Rinse well in running water and dry in the fresh air out of the sun.

Use up old yarns by crocheting squares. It's handy to have some ready to dye when you need them. By adjusting the size of the squares to cover a cushion, making them in contrasting colors, and then dyeing them one at a time in leftover tea to get subtly different shades, you can sew them together to get an interesting cushion cover. Here, the central square was dyed and fixed with iron acetate, while the others were fixed with burnt alum.

Earl Grey Tea

Earl Grey tea has a powerful aroma but it's a very calming drink. With essence of bergamot added to china or ceylon tea, it's the most famous of the flavored teas. You can appreciate the aroma of the dark orange tea with milk added, and dyeing with it is a pleasant experience.

You Will Need...

Crocheted squares (100% cotton)
.... 18 (approx. 80 g/2.8 oz)

For dyeing:
Earl Grey tea bags ... 12 (approx. 24 g/0.8 oz)
Burnt alum (for 16 squares)
.... 3 teaspoons (about 3 g/0.1 oz)
Iron acetate (for 2 squares)
.... scant 1/2 teaspoon (about 1 g/0.05 oz)

Equipment:
Pan (6-liter/6.5-qt), chopsticks or tongs, mesh bag, rubber band

Quantities Guide
Proportional to weight of materials to be dyed:

Earl Grey tea	Water
30%	40 times

Mordant (burnt alum)
Dissolved in a little hot water

For cotton or linen....................................5%
For silk or wool 3%

Mordant (iron acetate)

For cotton or linen....................................5%
For silk or wool 3%

Tips

• If using loose tea, use fillable teabags, if available, or a muslin bag.

• When using new yarn, the weight of tea required is 40% of the weight of the squares.

• If using wool, a pan must be used in Step 5 and the wool must be heated. Bring the pan to the boil, then turn off the heat and leave to cool.

• After rinsing with water in Step 6, simmering once more in dyeing solution will give a stronger color.

 1 teaspoon = 2.5 ml

1 Crocheting Squares

Make 18 crocheted squares.
See p. 68 for instructions. (Crocheting diagrams p. 66)

2 Preparation

• Weigh the squares and prepare the tea needed.

• Soak the squares in water and squeeze out excess water.

3 Making the Dyeing Solution

Place the teabags and 1.5 liters/3 pints of water in a pan, bring to the boil over a medium heat, then turn down heat. Simmer over a low heat for 10 minutes, and turn off heat. When cool, remove the teabags and add water to make up the dyeing solution to 3.2 liters/6.75 pints.

pull off tea bag labels

simmer for 10 minutes

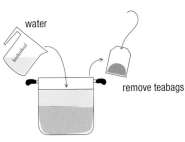

water

remove teabags

make up to 3.2 liters/6.75 pints

4 Dyeing

• When the dyeing solution is cool, put in the wet squares and mix well. Bring to the boil over a medium heat, then simmer for 10 minutes over a low heat, stirring occasionally.

• Turn off heat, and leave for 1 hour to cool. Move the squares around in the solution from time to time to prevent streaking.

simmer for 10 minutes

5 Fixing to Make 2 Colors

• Remove squares from the pan and rinse.

• Put 16 of them in a bowl of fixing solution of burnt alum stirred into 2 liters/4 pints of water, and the other 2 in a bowl with the iron-based fixing solution made with 400 ml/0.8 pint of water. Leave both for 30 minutes.

soak for 30 minutes

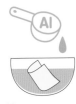 

• 16 squares:
water......... 2 liters/4 pints
burnt alum
.... 3 teaspoons
(about 3 g/0.1 oz)
dissolved in hot water

• 2 squares:
water........400 ml/0.8 pint
iron acetate scant
.... 1/2 teaspoon
(about 1 g/0.05 oz)

6 Rinsing and Drying

Rinse well in running water and spin lightly. Re-shape the squares and dry in the fresh air, out of the sun.

7 Making the Cushion Cover

See p. 68 for instructions.

I dyed some silk and wool in a third of a bottle of leftover red wine. Don't just keep leftover wine for cooking—remember there's another way you can enjoy using it!

For dyeing instructions see p. 61.

Red Wine

It goes without saying that the best thing to do with wine is drink it! But it's made from large quantities of grapes and so makes a good dye. Just as the taste varies according to where it has come from, so the dyeing results will be subtly different each time. To obtain this beautiful color, the secret is not to simmer for long but to soak for a long time.

Red Wine-Dyed Spectacles Case
(Instructions for making the spectacles case are on p. 80.)

	Burnt alum	Iron acetate	Copper mordant
Cotton			
Silk			
Wool			

WINTER

Kitchen Dyeing for Winter

When the weather's cold, a warm kitchen is the most comfortable place to be. I spend longer over cooking, which makes the family happy. But while I'm cooking I tend to think, "What if I used that for dyeing…?" and I often get distracted.

Black soybeans are a prime example. Just when I'm busy with preparations for New Year celebrations I find myself wanting to dye. The kitchen is full of potential dye colors. So be ready to dye whenever you cook. Steam rising from pans on the hob feels good on the skin in the winter.

I dyed one sleeve of an old Aran sweater together with some printed cotton and used them to make this little drawstring bag. Pull it open and you see the pretty floral print of the coordinating cotton lining. The bag seems small, but the knitted fabric stretches and it can hold a surprising amount.

Orange Peel

In Japan, winter would not be winter without mandarin oranges, the country's most popular fruit. If you chop up the peel and keep it on newspaper to dry out, you have an excellent resource for dyeing. It produces rather pale shades, so the weight of peel used should be 3 to 5 times the weight of the items to be dyed.

You Will Need...

Sleeve from Aran sweater (100% wool)
.... approx. 20 x 18 cm/8 x 7 in
(about 70 g/2.5 oz)
Lining fabric (100% cotton)
.... approx. 45 x 25 cm/18 x 10 in
(about 15 g/0.5 oz)

For dyeing:
Orange peel................................ 250 g/9 oz
Copper mordant
................3.5 teaspoons (about 8.5 g/0.3 oz)

Equipment:
Pan (6.5-liter/7-qt), chopsticks or tongs, rubber gloves, 2 x mesh bags, 2 x rubber bands

Quantities Guide
Proportional to weight of materials to be dyed:

Orange peel	Water
3 times	45 times

Mordant (copper mordant)

For cotton or linen..................... approx. 15%
For silk or wool .... approx. 10%

Change the mordant to change the shade

Using iron acetate as a mordant gives beige. See photo of mini tote on this page.

For cotton or linen...................... approx. 5%
For silk or wool .... approx. 3%

Tips

- Due to the quantity of orange peel, better results may come from dividing it between 2 mesh bags.
- Any sort of citrus fruit can be used for dyeing.

Aran sweaters have gone out of fashion, but here's a way of re-using yours.

1 Preparation

Cut a sleeve out of the sweater, soak it in warm water together with the lining fabric, and spin lightly.

2 Making the Dyeing Solution

 Use orange peel that has been cut up into small pieces and left to dry at room temperature for at least 10 days.

Put the orange peel in 1 or more mesh bags, add to 3 liters/6 pints of water in a pan and bring to the boil. Simmer for 15 minutes, then turn off heat. When cool, remove the orange peel and add water to make up the dyeing solution to 3.8 liters/7.5 pints.

simmer for 15 minutes

3 Dyeing and Fixing

When the dyeing solution is cool add copper mordant and stir well. Put in the wet items for dyeing and agitate until they absorb the dyeing solution. Place over a medium heat, bring to the boil, simmer over low heat for 10 minutes and turn off heat. Leave to cool for one hour.

stir occasionally
to avoid streaks

simmer for 10 minutes

---

4 Rinsing and Drying

Rinse the items in running water, spin lightly and dry in the fresh air, out of the sun.

5 Making the Bag

See p. 82 for instructions.

Fixing with iron acetate gives a beige shade. While dyeing I felted some wool and made a cute mini tote. See p. 83 for instructions.

I always have leftover balls of wool from knitting projects. With three balls of single-colored wool I used two types of mordant to create wool with three shades. The basic colors were brick red, off white and pale blue. The single color turns into something unique with the wool dyed in lighter and darker shades.

Marigolds

Marigolds fill parks and gardens with colorful displays in yellow and orange from May till late autumn. Tea made from marigold petals is sold by herbalists as a beauty treatment, and both the petals and the tea make good materials for dyeing. Dry some yellow and orange flowers and have them ready to use.

You Will Need...

Single-color wool
(mix of 53% alpaca/wool/nylon)
.... 2 balls (80 g/2.8 oz)

For dyeing:
Dried marigold flowers................... 30 g/1 oz
Burnt alum
.... 2.5 teaspoons (approx. 2.5 g/0.1 oz)
Iron acetate
.....................1 teaspoon (about 2.5 g/0.1 oz)

Equipment:
Pan (6-liter/6.5-qt), chopsticks or tongs, mesh bag, rubber band, plastic parcel tape, fabric conditioner

Quantities Guide
Proportional to weight of materials to be dyed:

Dried marigold flowers	Water
40%	45 times

Mordant (burnt alum)

 Dissolved in a little hot water

For cotton or linen....................................5%
For silk or wool 3%

Mordant (iron acetate)

For cotton or linen....................................5%
For silk or wool 3%

Tips

- Dyeing white wool with marigold gives a yellow with burnt alum or a khaki-brown with iron acetate. If you use colored wool you can get some surprising color combinations.
- 10~12 fresh marigold flowers produces about 5 g/0.2 oz of dried petals.

1 Preparation

Wind wool into 2 skeins about 50 cm/20 in long.

50cm

Bind tightly with plastic tape, leaving no gaps, for 4~5 cms/2 in in 3 places to retain the original color. Bind a second layer on top, going back to the start, and tie the ends of the tape together. See p. 84 for details.

Soak the wool thoroughly in warm water.

2 Making the Dyeing Solution

Place the marigold flowers in a mesh bag, place in a pan with 2 liters/4 pints of water and heat. When it comes to the boil, turn down heat, simmer for 10 minutes, and then turn off heat.

add water

remove bag

When cool, remove the bag and add water to make up the dyeing solution to 3.5 liters/ 7 pints.

turn off heat

3 Dyeing and Fixing

 Add dissolved burnt alum to the dyeing solution.

Put in the wool skeins and place over a medium heat. Bring to the boil and simmer over low heat for 10 minutes then turn off heat and leave to cool. When cool, rinse thoroughly in warm running water and spin lightly.

Bind the skeins of wool further in the same way for 6~7 cm/2.5 in widths in 2 locations (see p. 84 for details). Add iron acetate mordant to 3 liters/6 pints of warm water in a pan, put in the wool and bring to the boil over medium heat. Simmer over low heat for 10 minutes and then leave to cool.

4 Rinsing and Drying

When cool, squeeze out water and remove tapes. Rinse the wool thoroughly in warm running water, then soak in warm water containing fabric conditioner.

Spin lightly and dry in the fresh air, out of the sun.

5 Knitting the Scarf

See p. 84 for instructions.

I came across an old linen handkerchief with a Chinese lace border that took me back to my young days.

I dyed the handkerchief and some rayon ribbon to make a little wrapper for bread. The linen I used for the base fabric is the color achieved using iron-based mordant. You can use any fabric you like for an individual effect.

Rooibos Tea

Bread Wrapper from Linen Handkerchief
(Instructions for making the bread wrapper are on p. 81.)

See p. 57 for dyeing instructions.

Rooibos is a plant in the bean family that grows in the Cederberg mountains of South Africa. Its needle-shaped leaves are chopped finely to make this unusual tea. Used for dyeing with copper-based mordant, it gives a bright yellow color reminiscent of gingko trees in autumn.

I dyed a little gauze bag to make pretty gift wrapping.

The solution left over after I dyed some felt I used again to dye *washi* paper, which I soaked first.

Felt is made of wool but also contains rayon, so when I dyed some felt and wool together, the felt turned out a lighter, softer shade. With burnt alum I got a pink beige and iron acetate gave me gray with a hint of purple. By folding the felt and sewing it all around with blanket stitch I made a simple pouch.

Black Soybeans

Felt Accessory Case
(Instructions for making the accessory case are on p. 85.)

See p. 62 for dyeing instructions.

Black soybeans are eaten in Japan as a special dish for the New Year. A rusty nail is added to the pot when the beans are boiled to help preserve their lustrous black color. The black cooking water is rich in anthocyanins, which give plants red and purple pigmentation, and used with iron-based mordant it gives a pale purple shade. Black soybean tea does not produce much color, so it's better to dye with black soybean cooking water.

These oven mitts double as mats to stand hot pans on

When I tidy my kitchen drawers I find fabrics I can dye…

Oven mitts get merciless use, so I made some from old kitchen towels that wouldn't matter. Dyeing some floral printed fabric at the same time to use for contrast makes them a little bit special. Places where I had bleached out stains created some patchiness, but this, too, has its own charm.

Mixed Herbs

Oven Mitts from Kitchen Towels
(Instructions for making the oven mitts are on p. 86.)

See p. 63 for dyeing instructions.

A seasoning that mixes thyme, sage, rosemary, basil, marjoram and savory is a precious resource because it contains all the herbs essential to Mediterranean cooking. Herbs give soft colors when used for dyeing. Try putting together all the out-of-date dried herbs you find in your cupboard.

I made a large square crocheting each row with a different textured yarn. The dark brown row from wool dyed with iron-based mordant gives an accent.

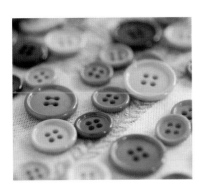

Using coffee alone, plastic buttons can be dyed all sorts of shades. I made a pot holder by using overcast stitch to sew together four small crocheted squares.

See p. 64 for dyeing instructions.

Coffee

Crocheted Pot Holders
(Instructions for making the pot holders are on p. 69.)

You can dye with coffee beans, but I recommend using instant coffee. Simply dissolving it makes an instant dyeing solution and you can cut out the simmering process and save time. Instant coffee is highly concentrated so just a little makes a strong dye. Whatever mordant you use, you'll get beige or brown shades.

	Burnt alum	Iron acetate	Copper mordant
Cotton			
Silk			
Wool			

Not just apple tea but any sort of black tea can be used without a mordant to give fabric this antique look. I had a cotton shirt that was out-of-date, but I was fond of the pin tucks so I decided to use it for an outfit cover. In addition, I cut off the sleeves and ran elastic through the tops to make a pair of arm covers. I dyed some pretty lace at the same time, and sewed it round the cuffs.

I cut out the parts I needed and dyed them.

I made a pattern that fitted the hanger.

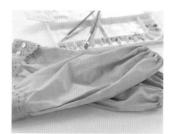

Iron-based mordant gave a pinkish gray.

I also dyed some lace and sewed it to the cuffs for added flair.

Apple Tea

Outfit Cover from Recycled Blouse
(Instructions for making the outfit cover are on p. 87.)

See p. 57 for dyeing instructions.

Delicious French apple tea is a ceylon tea flavored with green apple. I had some that was past its use-by date so I used it for dyeing. While dyeing I enjoyed its sweet, refreshing fragrance. Iron-based mordant gives a beautiful pinkish gray.

I had a pale pink linen blouse that I no longer wore, but it had such delicate hand-stitching on it that I couldn't throw it away. So I tried dyeing it using nine teabags, to turn it into something else. I decided which parts of the blouse I would need before I started, and in this case I dyed the back and sleeves to make a bag. I added some handmade decoration to give it more appeal.

Oolong Tea

Bag from Recycled Blouse
(Instructions for making the bag are on p. 87.)

See p. 57 for dyeing instructions.

Oolong tea is a popular Chinese tea made of half-fermented tea leaves. Teabags are inexpensive, which is an added plus for dyeing. The resulting shades are the same sort of earthy colors as for other teas. Iron-based mordant gives a soft gray.

Green Tea

(photo p. 21)

Knitted Silk Drawstring Bags
(Instructions for making bags are on p. 70.)

You Will Need…

Old silk fabric (100% silk)
.................................38 x 170 cm/15 x 67 in
Silk thread ....2.5 m/2.75 yd
.... total weight 35 g/1.25 oz

For dyeing:
Green tea.................................... 20 g/0.7 oz
Iron acetate
...... scant 1/2 teaspoon (approx. 1 g/0.05 oz)

Equipment:
Pan (3.5-liter/4-qt), chopsticks or tongs,
2 fillable teabags or muslin bags

Quantities Guide
Proportional to weight of materials to be dyed:

Green tea	Water
60%	50 times
Mordant (iron acetate)	

For cotton or linen.....................................5%
For silk or wool 3%

Change the mordant to change the shade

Using burnt alum or copper mordant instead of iron acetate in Step 3 gives different colors.

- Add 1 teaspoon (about 1 g/0.05 oz) of burnt alum to the dyeing solution to get a soft yellow.
- Add 1 heaped teaspoon (about 2.8 g/ 0.1 oz) of copper mordant to the dyeing solution for a yellow gold.

1 Preparation

Soak the fabric and thread in water, then squeeze out excess water.

Divide the green tea between the 2 teabags and fill loosely.

2 Making the Dyeing Solution

Place the green tea bags with 1 liter/2 pints of water into a pan over a medium heat. When it comes to the boil reduce heat and simmer for 10 minutes. Turn off the heat and leave to cool. When cool, remove the green tea and add water to make up the solution to 1.7 liters/3.5 pints.

simmer for 10 minutes

make up to 1.7 liters/3.5 pints

	Burnt alum	Iron acetate	Copper mordant
Cotton			
Silk			
Wool			

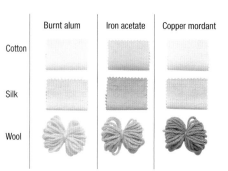

3 Dyeing and Fixing

- Add a scant half teaspoon of iron acetate to the dyeing solution and stir well.
- Put in the wet fabric and thread and swirl them around so they absorb the dyeing solution. Place pan over a medium heat and when it boils turn off the heat.
- Leave to cool for about 1 hour, stirring occasionally

(For fabrics other than silk, simmer for 10 minutes in the dyeing solution)

Burnt alum or copper mordant can be used instead of iron acetate for color variations. The dyeing process is the same.

4 Rinsing and Drying

Rinse thoroughly in running water, spin lightly and dry in the fresh air, out of the sun.

5 Making the Drawstring Bags

See p. 70 for instructions.

Other Ways to Dye with Tea

The dyeing procedure is the same as for green tea on p. 56, and the same equipment is used.

Hibiscus Tea
(photo p. 20)

Small Sewing Accessories
(Instructions for making the accessories are on p. 67)

Tips

- Boil the hibiscus tea, simmer for 1 minute and turn off heat. Make dyeing solution up to 600 ml/20 fl oz, then divide into two quantities of 400 ml/ 13.5 fl oz and 200 ml/6.5 fl oz.
- Add iron acetate (or copper mordant) to 400 ml/13.5 fl oz of solution and burnt alum to 200 ml/6.5 fl oz of solution, then follow the procedure in Step 3 on p. 56.

You Will Need...

For the pin cushion:
Knitting wool (white) .... 14 m/15 yd
Embroidery thread (white).......... 8 m/8.75 yd
(fixed with iron acetate)
Knitting wool (white) .... 6 m/6.5 yd
Knitting wool (mohair; white) .... 2 m/2.2 yd
(fixed with burnt alum)
.... Total weight approx. 12 g/0.4 oz

For dyeing:
Hibiscus tea.................................. 6 g/0.2 oz
Iron acetate
.............1/3 teaspoon (approx. 0.8 g/0.03 oz)
Burnt alum
.......scant 1 teaspoon (approx. 0.8 g/0.03 oz)

Quantities Guide
Proportional to weight of materials to be dyed:

Hibiscus tea	Water
50%	50 times

Change the mordant to change the shade.

For copper mordant 1/2 teaspoon (approx. 1.2 g/0.04 oz) in 400 ml/13.5 fl oz water

Rooibos Tea
(photo p. 50)

Bread Wrapper from Linen Handkerchief
(Instructions for making the bread wrapper are on p. 81)

Tips

- Follow the dyeing procedure on p. 56.
- Of the ribbons of synthetic fibers, only nylon and rayon can be dyed.

You Will Need...

Handkerchief (100% linen)
......................................30 cm/12 in square
Rayon ribbon (7 mm/0.25 in)
.... 140 cm/1.5 yd
total weight 12 g/0.4 oz

For dyeing:
Rooibos tea.................................. 6 g/0.2 oz
Copper mordant
.............3/4 teaspoon (approx. 1.8 g/0.08 oz)

Quantities Guide
Proportional to weight of materials to be dyed:

Rooibos tea	Water
50%	50 times
Mordant (copper mordant)	

Oolong Tea
(photo p. 55)

Bag from Recycled Blouse
(Instructions for making the bag are on p. 87)

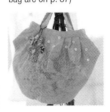

Tips

- Follow the dyeing procedure on p. 56.
- If using silk or wool, the weight of tea should be 50% of the weight of the fabric.

You Will Need...

Blouse parts (100% linen)
.... 2 pieces x 40 x 50 cm/15.75 x 19.75 in
weight approx. 50 g/1.75 oz

For dyeing:
Oolong tea .... 45 g/1.6 oz
Burnt alum
.... 2 teaspoons (approx. 2 g/0.1 oz)

Quantities Guide
Proportional to weight of materials to be dyed:

Oolong tea	Water
90%	50 times
Mordant (copper mordant)	

For cotton or linen....................................4%
For silk or wool 2%

Apple Tea
(photo p. 54)

Outfit Cover from Recycled Blouse
(Instructions for making the outfit cover are on p. 87)

Tips

- No mordant is needed when dyeing with apple tea or other black teas.
- After boiling, simmer for 10 minutes and make the dyeing solution up to 3.5 liters/7 pints.
- Add pre-wettened items, bring to boil and simmer over low heat for 5 minutes.
- Leave to cool, removing cotton lawn earlier because it's a finer fabric and dyes quickly.

You Will Need...

Yoke section of shirt (100% cotton)............1
Cotton lawn (100% cotton)
.................................90 x 50 cm/35 x 20 in
Torchon lace (1.8 cm/0.7 in) .... 2 m/2.2 yd
total weight approx. 70 g/2.5 oz

For dyeing:
Apple tea (or other black tea)
.... 28 g/1 oz

Quantities Guide
Proportional to weight of materials to be dyed:

Oolong tea	Water
40%	50 times

For cotton or linen....................................15%
For silk or wool 10%

1 teaspoon = 2.5 ml

Spices
(photo p. 22)

Embroidered Cloth Wrapper
(Instructions for making the cloth are on p. 74.)

You Will Need...

For the cloth:
Linen cloth
.........50 cm/20 in square (approx. 60 g/2 oz)

For dyeing:
Fine ground pepper....................90 g/3.2 oz
Burnt alum.....3 teaspoons (about 3 g/0.1 oz)

Equipment:
Pan (6-liter/6.5-qt), chopsticks or tongs,
mesh bag, rubber band

Quantities Guide
Proportional to weight of materials to be dyed:

Pepper	Water
1.5 times	45 times

Mordant (burnt alum)	
	5% of fabric dissolved in a little hot water

For embroidery thread:

No. 25 embroidery thread (white)
.........................3 skeins (approx. 6 g/0.2 oz)

For dyeing:
Cloves ....12 g/0.4 oz
Burnt alum ....1 teaspoon (about 1 g/0.05 oz)
Iron acetate
.........scant 1/2 teaspoon (about 1 g/0.05 oz)
Copper mordant
..............scant 1 teaspoon (about 2 g/0.1 oz)

Equipment:
Pan (1.5-liter/3-pint), 3 x 500 ml/17 fl oz
bowls, chopsticks or tongs, fillable teabags
or muslin bags

Quantities Guide
Proportional to weight of materials to be dyed:

Cloves	Water
2 times...	100 times

Mordant (3 types)		

The thread is light in weight, so calculate
from the quantity of water.
Quantities given above are for 300 ml/
10 fl oz of water.

How to Dye the Embroidery Thread

1 Preparation

Make each skein of thread
about 15 cm/6 in long and
tie in the ends with
separate thread. Soak in
hot water for 20 minutes,
then rinse.

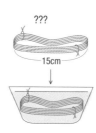

2 Making the Dyeing Solution

Put the cloves in the bag and put in the pan with 800
ml/1.6 pints of water. Bring to the boil, turn heat to low
and simmer for 10 minutes. When cool, take out the
cloves. There should be about 600 ml/1.2 pints of
dyeing solution.

3 Dyeing the Threads

Put the 3 skeins of
embroidery thread into
the dyeing solution and
swirl about. Bring to the
boil over medium heat,
then turn down heat and
simmer for 10 minutes.
Leave to cool, stirring
occasionally. When
completely cool, rinse and
separate the 3 skeins.

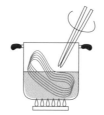

simmer for 10 minutes

4 Fixing the Dye

Put 300 ml/10 fl oz of cold or warm water in each of 3
bowls, and stir in burnt alum, iron acetate or copper
mordant to make 3 fixing solutions. Put 1 skein of dyed
thread in each, swirl about so that the solution fully
penetrates, and leave for 30 minutes.

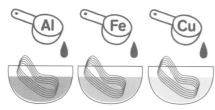

Burnt alum   Iron acetate   Copper mordant

5 Rinsing and Drying

Taking care that the thread does not get tangled, rinse
each skein in running water, squeeze out excess water,
re-shape and dry in the fresh air, out of the sun.

How to Dye the Cloth

1 Making the Dyeing Solution

Put the pepper in a mesh bag and put in a pan with
1.5 liters/3 pints of water. Bring it to the boil and
simmer on a low heat for 15 minutes. Turn off the heat,
allow to cool, remove the pepper and add water to
make up the dyeing solution to 2.7 liters/5.75 pints.

(Unused cloth is more difficult to dye, so simmer in this
dyeing solution for about 5 minutes, allow to cool, spin
lightly and continue to Step 2.)

2 Dyeing and Fixing

When the dyeing solution is cool add burnt alum
dissolved in hot water, put in the wet linen cloth and
swirl about. Bring to the boil and simmer over a low
heat for 10 minutes. Leave to cool for 1 hour, stirring
occasionally.

3 Rinsing and Drying

Rinse in running water, spin lightly and dry in the fresh
air, out of the sun.
See p. 74 for instructions to make the wrapper.

Quantities for dyeing
(as proportion of basket weight):
Powdered cinnamon 50%
Water... 50 times
Burnt alum..5%
(If using iron acetate 5%)

Main Points for Dyeing Baskets

When making the dyeing solution, powdered cinnamon
must be carefully strained, as with turmeric (see p. 27).
Immerse the basket fully in the hot dyeing solution,
using a weight to stop it floating if necessary. Allow to
cool, then rinse thoroughly in water, drain and dry.

You Will Need...

Torchon lace (4 cm/1.5 in) .... 2.2 m/2.4 yd
No. 25 embroidery thread (white)
.... 2 m/2.2 yd

For dyeing:
Gardenia seeds...........5 (about 10 g/0.35 oz)
Burnt alum.....1 teaspoon (about 1 g/0.05 oz)

Equipment:
Pan (1.8-liter/2-qt), chopsticks or tongs,
mesh bag, rubber band, rubber gloves

Quantities Guide
Proportional to weight of materials to be dyed:

Gardenia seeds	Water
50%	40 times

Mordant (burnt alum)
Dissolved in a little hot water

For cotton or linen.....................................5%
For silk or wool 3%

Tips

• Gardenia seeds swell, so ensure they have
plenty of space in the mesh bag.

1 Preparation

Soak the lace and thread in hot water for 30 minutes,
rinse and squeeze out excess water.

2 Making the Dyeing Solution

Put the gardenia seeds in a mesh bag and put in a pan
with 1 liter/2 pints of water. Bring to the boil, simmer
over a low heat for 10 minutes, and turn off heat. When
cool, remove the gardenia seeds. There should be about
800 ml/1.6 pints of dyeing solution.

medium heat

simmer over low heat for 10 minutes

cool

3 Dyeing and Fixing

When the dyeing solution is cool, add burnt alum
dissolved in hot water. Put in the lace and thread and
stir. Bring to the boil over a medium heat, then simmer
over low heat for 10 minutes and turn off heat. Leave to
cool for one hour, stirring occasionally.

medium heat

simmer for 10 minutes over low heat

4 Rinsing and Drying

Rinse the lace and thread in running water and spin
lightly. Reshape and dry in the fresh air, out of the sun.

5 Making the Tablecloth and Glass Holders

See p. 81 for instructions.

1 teaspoon = 2.5 ml

Purple Perilla
(photo p. 34)

You Will Need...

Small napkins (linen 100%)
.... x 2 (about 15 g/0.5 oz)

For dyeing:
Purple perilla leaves.................... 75 g/2.6 oz
80% acetic acid........................30 ml/1 fl oz

Equipment:
Pan (3.5-liter/4-qt), chopsticks or tongs, mesh bag, rubber band, thick rubber gloves

Quantities Guide
Proportional to weight of materials to be dyed:

Purple perilla	Water
5 times	60 times

Mordant (80% acetic acid)

 per 1 liter/2 pints of dyeing solution

For cotton or linen..................... 30 ml/1 fl oz
For silk 20 ml/0.7
(Wool cannot be dyed in this low temperature process)

Tips

• This acid-fixed color will change if washed in an alkaline detergent. Wash napkins with neutral detergent and dry in a shaded location. Do not use a hot iron.

Recipe for Purple Perilla Juice

This makes a sweet, sharp-tasting concentrated juice. Add ice cubes and dilute to taste.

Ingredients for 5~6 glasses:
Purple perilla leaves.............. 50 g/1.75 oz
Sugar.................................... 120 g/4.25 oz
Table vinegar .... 60 ml/2 fl oz
Water................................. 300 ml/10 fl oz

❶ Boil the water and add finely chopped perilla leaves.

❷ Bring to boil and remove leaves.

❸ Add sugar and vinegar to taste, bring to boil once more, then turn off heat and leave to cool.

(When the vinegar is added the juice turns pink.)

Transfer to empty bottle or other container and store in the refrigerator.

---

1 Preparation

• Soak the napkins in hot water for 20 minutes, rinse and squeeze out excess water.

• Rinse the perilla leaves if they are dirty.

2 Making the Dyeing Solution

Chop the perilla leaves finely, put in a mesh bag and put in a pan with 1 liter/2 pints of water. Bring to the boil and turn off heat after 1 minute.

simmer for 1 minute

Remove the leaves and add the acetic acid. The solution will turn red.

turns red

---

3 Dyeing the Napkins

Put the napkins in the red dyeing solution and place over a low heat. Wearing thick rubber gloves, work the solution through the fabric until it gets too hot. Turn off the heat, put a lid on the pan and leave to cool, stirring occasionally.

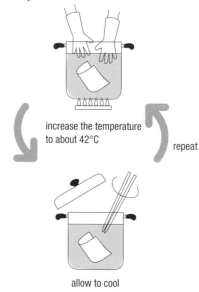

increase the temperature to about 42°C

repeat

allow to cool

When cool, repeat this procedure and leave overnight to cool.

leave overnight

(Silk is easier to dye, and should be soaked 2~4 hours.)

4 Rinsing and Drying

Rinse in running water and dry in the fresh air, out of the sun.

Red Wine
(photo p. 44)

Spectacles Case
(Instructions for making the spectacles case are on p. 80.)

You Will Need...

Outer fabric (100% silk)
....20 cm/8 in square
Lining fabric (100% wool)
....20 cm/8 in square
No. 25 embroidery thread (white)
.... 2 m/2.2 yd
total weight 12 g/0.4 oz

For dyeing:
Red wine ....250 ml/8.5 fl oz
Burnt alum.....1 teaspoon (about 1 g/0.05 oz)

Equipment:
Pan (1.5-liter/3-pint), chopsticks or tongs, rubber gloves

Quantities Guide
Proportional to weight of materials to be dyed:

Red wine	Water
20%	40 times

Mordant (burnt alum)	
	Dissolved in a little hot water

For cotton or linen.................................10%
For silk or wool 8%

Tips

- Silk is particularly recommended for dyeing with red wine.
- When dyeing cotton, a better effect is achieved with cotton with a satin finish.

1 Preparation

Soak the fabrics and thread thoroughly in warm water, rinse and squeeze out excess water.

2 Making Dyeing Solution and Pre-Soaking Fabrics

Solution and Pre-Soaking Fabrics
Put together 250 ml/8.5 fl oz of red wine and 250 ml/8.5 fl oz of water to make 500 ml/1 pint of dyeing solution.

500 ml/1 pint

Put in fabrics and thread, stir, heat to about 40°C and turn off heat. Leave to soak for 1 hour, stirring occasionally.

soak for 1 hour

3 Dyeing and Fixing

Take fabric and thread out of the pan. Add dissolved burnt alum to the dyeing solution and return the fabric and thread. Place over a low heat, bring to the boil and turn off heat. Leave to soak for 1 hour, stirring occasionally. (If using cotton or linen, return to heat once again, bring to boil, turn off heat and leave to soak for 1 hour.)

soak for 1 hour

4 Rinsing and Drying

Rinse materials thoroughly in warm running water, squeeze out excess water and dry in the fresh air, out of the sun.

5 Making the Spectacles Case

See p. 80 for instructions.

1 teaspoon = 2.5 ml

Black Soybeans
(photo p. 51)

Felt Accessory Case
(Instructions for making the accessory case are on p. 85.)

You Will Need...

Felt (40% wool, 60% rayon)
.....................................10 x 24 cm/4 x 9.5 in
Knitting yarn (100% wool)
...............4 m/4.4 yd (fixed with iron acetate)
.... 1 m/1.1 yd (fixed with burnt alum)
total weight 8 g/0.25 oz

For dyeing:
Black soybean cooking water
....500 ml/17 fl oz
Iron acetate (for felt and 4 m/4.4 yd of yarn)
.... scant 1/2 teaspoon (about 1 g/0.05 oz)
Black soybean cooking water ..200 ml/7 fl oz
Burnt alum (for 1 m/1.1 yd of yarn)
.............1/3 teaspoon (approx. 0.3 g/0.01 oz)

Equipment:
Pan (1.5-liter/3-pint), small pan (600-ml/
1-qt), chopsticks or tongs, rubber gloves

Quantities Guide
Proportional to weight of materials to be dyed:

Black soybean cooking water	Water
60 times	60 times

Mordant (iron acetate)

For cotton or linen.....................................5%
For silk or wool 3%
For the remaining 200 ml/7 fl oz of cooking
water, use burnt alum as a fixative and dye
1 m/1.1 yd of yarn a contrasting shade. For
200 ml/7 fl oz of liquid, use 0.3 g/0.01 oz of
mordant.

Tips

• Using the same method but substituting
burnt alum as the mordant gives a
contrasting shade.

Mordant (burnt alum)

dissolved in a little hot water

For cotton or linen....................................5%
For silk or wool 3%

1 Preparation

Soak the wool and yarn thoroughly in warm water for
20 minutes, rinse and squeeze out excess water.

2 Simmering Materials in the Dyeing Solution

Put the felt in a pan with 500 ml/17 fl oz of black
soybean cooking water warmed to about 30°C, and
wearing rubber gloves work it well so that the solution
penetrates the felt. Bring to the boil over a medium
heat, turn off heat and allow to cool.
(Take care not to simmer, as the pigment deteriorates.)

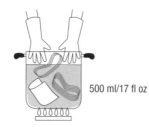
500 ml/17 fl oz

bring to boil and turn off heat

3 Dyeing and Fixing

When cool, remove the materials. Put 200 ml/7 fl oz of
fresh black soybean cooking water in a small pan, stir
in 1/3 teaspoon of burnt alum and put in 1 m/1.1 yd of
yarn. Stir in 1/2 teaspoon of iron acetate to the original
pan and return the felt and 4 m/4.4 yd of yarn. Put both
pans over medium heat, bring to the boil and turn off
heat. Allow to cool, stirring occasionally.

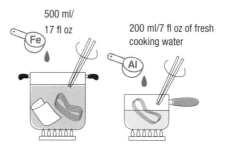
500 ml/17 fl oz

200 ml/7 fl oz of fresh
cooking water

bring to boil and turn off heat

4 Rinsing and Drying

Add water of the same temperature to the materials in
the 2 pans to wash out excess color, then rinse, spin
lightly and dry in the fresh air out of the sun.

5 Making the Accessory Case

See p. 85 for instructions.

Recipe for Cooking Black Soybeans

This is how I cook black soybeans, leaving the
liquid to use in dyeing.

Ingredients for 5~6 glasses:
Ingredients:
Black soybeans...................................250 g/9 oz
Sugar.............250 g/9 oz (same weight as beans)
Water.....1.2 liters/2.5 pints (5 x volume of beans)
Rusty nail

❶ Soak the soybeans in 1.2 liters/2.5 pints of
water overnight (12 hours).

❷ Bring the beans to the boil over a low heat,
turn off the heat and leave to cool for
4~5 hours. Strain the beans and discard
700 ml/1.5 pints of cooking water. (This can
be used for dyeing)

❸ Add fresh water and a rusty nail to the beans
and simmer until soft.

❹ Make a syrup by dissolving 250 gm/9 oz of
sugar in 400 ml/14 fl oz of water. Strain the
cooked beans, add them to the syrup and
bring to the boil before turning off heat.
(This cooking water can also be used for
dyeing, but because it contained a rusty nail,
only iron-based mordant can be used.)

❺ Leave the beans in the syrup for a further
24 hours.

Mixed Herbs
(photo p. 52)

Oven Mitts from Kitchen Towels
(Instructions for making the oven mitts are on p. 86.)

You Will Need...

Waffle cloth (100% cotton)
....................................30 x 36 cm/12 x 14 in
Linen fabric (100% linen)
....................................12 x 20 cm/4.5 x 8 in

For dyeing:
Mixed herbs.................................. 60 g/2 oz
Iron acetate generous
................1/2 teaspoon (about 1.5 g/0.05 oz)

Equipment:
Pan (3.5-liter/4-qt), chopsticks or tongs,
mesh bag, rubber band, rubber gloves

Quantities Guide
Proportional to weight of materials to be dyed:

Mixed herbs	Water
50%	50 times

Mordant (iron acetate)

For cotton or linen....................................5%
For silk or wool 3%

Tips

- Well-used kitchen towels can be dyed very successfully.
- Using the same method with burnt alum as the mordant gives a contrasting shade.

1 Preparation

Soak the fabrics and squeeze out excess water. Place the mixed herbs in a mesh bag and close with a rubber band.

2 Making the Dyeing Solution

Place herbs in a pan with 800 ml/1.7 pints of water and bring to the boil. Simmer over a low heat for 10 minutes, then turn off heat.

simmer for 10 minutes

When cool, remove the herbs and add water to make the dyeing solution up to 1.5 liters/3 pints.

make up to 1.5 liters/3 pints

3 Dyeing and Fixing

When cool, add iron acetate to the dyeing solution, stir well and add the fabrics. Place over a medium heat, bring to the boil and simmer over low heat for 10 minutes. Turn off heat and leave to cool for 1 hour, stirring occasionally. For lighter shades fabrics can be removed more quickly.

simmer for 10 minutes

4 Rinsing and Drying

When cool, rinse thoroughly in running water, spin lightly and dry in the fresh air, out of the sun.

5 Making the Oven Mitt

See p. 86 for instructions.

1 teaspoon = 2.5 ml

Coffee
(photo p. 53)

Dyeing yarns for 1 mid-sized pot holder (burnt alum) and
1 small pot holder (iron acetate)

Using coffee beans

Use half the quantity given for instant coffee, grind finely,
place in a fillable teabag or muslin bag and follow the
same instructions to make the dyeing solution.

You Will Need...

For mid-sized (1.5-liter/3-pint) pans:
Knitting wool............................... 22 m/24 yd
Silk thread .... 7 m/7.7 yd
Cotton thread............................... 3 m/3.3 yd
Mohair wool................................... 3 m/3.3 yd
        total weight approx. 12 g/0.4 oz

For dyeing:
Instant coffee............................. 12 g/0.4 oz
Burnt alum
...generous 1/2 teaspoon (approx. 0.6 g/0.02 oz)

Quantities Guide
Proportional to weight of materials to be dyed:

Instant coffee	Water
100%	60 times

Mordant (burnt alum)
Al   5%

You Will Need...

For small (1-liter/2-pint) pan:
Mohair wool................................... 3 m/3.3 yd
Knitting wool................................. 5 m/5.5 yd
Silk thread .... 1 m/1.1 yd
        total weight approx. 4 g/0.15 oz

For dyeing:
Instant coffee................................ 6 g/0.2 oz
Iron acetate
............1/5 teaspoon (approx. 0.5 g/0.02 oz)

Quantities Guide
Proportional to weight of materials to be dyed:

Instant coffee	Water
120%	70 times

Mordant (iron acetate)
Fe   Proportional to volume of water 0.5 g/0.02 oz per 300 ml/10 fl oz

Equipment (for both):
Chopsticks or tongs, rubber gloves
Iron acetate .... 1/5 tsp

---

1 Preparation

Wind wool into 15 cm/
6 in-length skeins.

Soak thoroughly in warm
water, rinse and squeeze
out excess water.

For mid-sized pan:
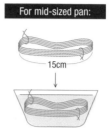
15cm

2 Making the Dyeing Solution

Put 700 ml/1.5 pints of
hot water in a pan and
stir in 12 g/0.4 oz of
instant coffee until it has
completely dissolved.

stir till dissolved

3 Dyeing and Fixing

When the dyeing solution is cool, add burnt alum
dissolved in hot water and stir. Add wool skeins and stir,
then place over low heat. Bring to the boil, simmer for
10 minutes, and turn off heat. Allow to cool, stirring
occasionally.

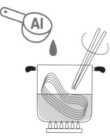
simmer for 10 minutes

---

1 Preparation

Wind wool into 15 cm/
6 in-length skeins.

Soak thoroughly in warm
water, rinse and squeeze
out excess water.

For small pan:
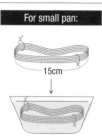
15cm

2 Making the Dyeing Solution

Pour 300 ml/10 fl oz of
hot water in a small pan
and stir in 6 g/0.2 oz of
instant coffee until it has
completely dissolved.

stir till dissolved

3 Dyeing and Fixing

When the dyeing solution is cool, add iron acetate and
stir. Add wool skeins and stir, then place over low heat.
When it comes to the boil, remove mohair and silk
skeins, simmer the wool skein for 10 minutes, and then
turn off heat. Allow to cool, stirring occasionally.

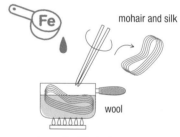
mohair and silk
wool
simmer for 10 minutes

---

4 Rinsing and Drying (both sizes)

Taking care to prevent wool from getting tangled, add
warm water to wash out excess dye. Rinse well,
squeeze out excess water, re-shape skeins and dry in
the fresh air, out of the sun.

5 Crocheting the Pot Holders (both sizes)

See p. 69 for instructions.

Sewing, Knitting and Crochet Instructions

SPRING

P.18 Teapot Mat and Coasters

See p. 19 for dyeing instructions

You Will Need...

Fine cotton stranded yarn
For teapot mat (1)
............approx. 8 g/0.3 oz (about 26 m)
For coaster (1)
.........approx. 4 g/0.15 oz (about 13 m)

Equipment:
2.0 mm crochet hook, wool needle

Teapot Mat

Make center ring, and crochet a granny square. Referring to the diagram on the right, crochet 6 rows. Finish the edge with slip stitch, and make a 5 cm/2 in loop in chain stitch. The completed square should be 11.5 cm/4.5 in square.

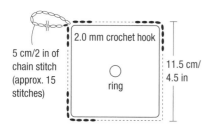

5 cm/2 in of chain stitch (approx. 15 stitches)

2.0 mm crochet hook

ring

11.5 cm/ 4.5 in

Coaster

In the same way as for the teapot mat, work from a center ring and crochet a granny square of 4 rows. Finish the edge with slip stitch (no loop needed). The finished size should be 8 cm/3.25 in square.

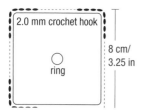

2.0 mm crochet hook

ring

8 cm/ 3.25 in

See p. 19 for dyeing instructions.

How to Crochet a Granny Square

This is a square crocheted in a pattern of chain stitch and double crochet, each row raised 3 chain stitches. The corners are formed using 2 chain stitches, with half double crochet to finish.

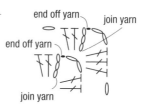

end off yarn   join yarn
end off yarn
join yarn

When using a different yarn for each row, finish with 2 chain stitches instead of half double crochet and a slip stitch onto the raised chain stitch.

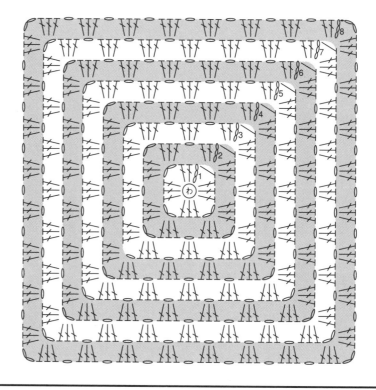

Making a Center Ring

end of yarn

❶ Wind the end of the yarn twice round forefinger to make a double circle.

❷ Release from finger and draw yarn through as shown.

❸ Wind yarn around hook again and draw it through.

❹ This makes the first stitch. Continue making stitches in the same way.

How to close the center ring (diagram shows single crochet)
Once you have the required number of stitches on the center ring, tighten it up.

end off yarn

a
b

When you have the required number of stitches, pull the end of the yarn a little. This tightens loop (a).

a
b

Pull loop (a) in the direction of the arrow, and tighten loop (b).

Thread the end of the yarn through the crochet on the reverse side to finish

After tightening loop (b), pull the end of the yarn to tighten loop (a).

66

P.20 Small Sewing Accessories

See p. 57 for dyeing instructions.

Pin Cushion

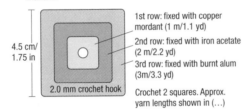

1st row: dyed mohair wool fixed with burnt alum (1 m/1.1 yd)

2nd row: dyed wool fixed with iron acetate (2 m/2.2 yd)

3rd row: dyed wool fixed with burnt alum (3m/3.3 yd)

4th row: dyed cotton fixed with iron acetate (4 m/4.4 yd)

5th row: dyed wool fixed with iron acetate (5 m/5.5 yd)

8.5 cm/ 3.5 in

4 cm/1.5 in of chain stitch (approx. 12 stitches)

Crochet 2 squares. Approx. yarn lengths shown in (…) (For overcast and chain stitch loop, about 1 m/1.1 yd of wool dyed with iron acetate mordant)

1 Crochet a Square

Crochet a granny square using yarns dyed three different shades (See p. 57). Following the diagram on p. 66, make a center ring, then crochet five rows using different yarn for each row, as shown. The finished square should be about 8.5 cm/3.5 in square. Make two.

2 Sew Together

Make a cushion in the same way as for the scissors tag below (without a cord). Sew the squares together with overcast stitch, insert the cushion and sew up. With remaining wool dyed with iron acetate mordant add a chain stitch loop.

Tag for Scissors

1 Crochet 2 Squares

Make a granny square using silk thread dyed 3 shades (See p. 57). Following the diagram on p. 66, make a center ring and crochet 3 rows in different colors. The finished size should be about 4.5 cm/1.75 in square. Make 2.

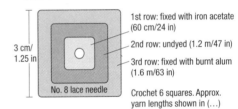

4.5 cm/ 1.75 in

1st row: fixed with copper mordant (1 m/1.1 yd)

2nd row: fixed with iron acetate (2 m/2.2 yd)

3rd row: fixed with burnt alum (3m/3.3 yd)

2.0 mm crochet hook

Crochet 2 squares. Approx. yarn lengths shown in (…)

2 Make the Cushion

Put silk fabric squares right sides together and sew together round the edge, leaving an opening. Turn, fill with wadding and sew up the opening.

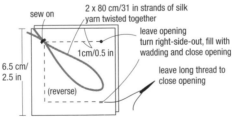

sew on

2 x 80 cm/31 in strands of silk yarn twisted together

leave opening turn right-side-out, fill with wadding and close opening

1cm/0.5 in

6.5 cm/ 2.5 in

(reverse)

leave long thread to close opening

3 Sew Squares Together

Put the 2 squares together with right sides out and sew together with overcast stitch (See p. 69). After sewing 3 sides, insert the cushion, draw out the cord at one corner, and close the remaining side.

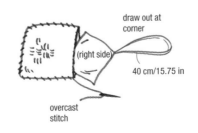

draw out at corner

(right side)

40 cm/15.75 in

overcast stitch

Book Mark

1 Crochet 6 Squares

Dye half the No. 8 embroidery thread in two shades (See p. 57) and leave the other half undyed. Make a center ring to crochet a granny square. Following the diagram on p. 66, crochet 3 rows in different colors. The finished size should be about 3 cm/1.25 in square. Make 6.

3 cm/ 1.25 in

1st row: fixed with iron acetate (60 cm/24 in)

2nd row: undyed (1.2 m/47 in)

3rd row: fixed with burnt alum (1.6 m/63 in)

No. 8 lace needle

Crochet 6 squares. Approx. yarn lengths shown in (…)

2 Sew Squares Together

With remaining undyed yarn, sew the squares together using overcast stitch. Finish the edge with slip stitch, continue making a cord in chain stitch and fix a button on the end.

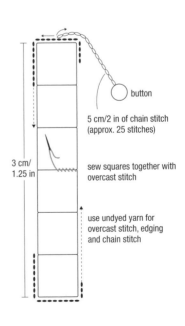

button

5 cm/2 in of chain stitch (approx. 25 stitches)

3 cm/ 1.25 in

sew squares together with overcast stitch

use undyed yarn for overcast stitch, edging and chain stitch

Pin Cushion

You Will Need...
Knitting wool (white)
..........................approx. 7 g/0.25 oz
(about 20m/22 yd)
Mohair knitting wool (white)
..........................approx. 2 g/0.05 oz
(about 2m/2.2 yd)
No. 5 embroidery thread (white)
..........................approx. 3 g/0.1 oz
(about 8m/8.75 yd)

Materials and equipment:
Wool fabric for cushions
.................2 x 10.5 cm/4.25 in square
Cotton wadding ....as required
3.0 mm crochet hook, wool needle, sewing needle and thread

Tag for Scissors

You Will Need...
Silk yarn
.... approx. 4 g/0.15 oz
(about 20 m/22 yd)

Materials and equipment:
Silk fabric for cushions
.....................2 x 6.5 cm/2.5 in square
Cotton wadding ....as required
2.0 mm crochet hook (or No. 0 lace needle), wool needle, sewing needle and thread

Book Mark

You Will Need...
No. 8 embroidery thread (ecru)
..............................approx. 35 m/38 yd

Materials and equipment:
Button............. 8 mm/0.25 in diameter
No. 8 lace needle, wool needle

P.42 Crocheted Cushion Cover

See p. 43 for dyeing instructions.

You Will Need...

Cotton slub yarn .. approx. 100 g/3.5 oz

Equipment:
Shell buttons
.................5 x 15 mm/0.5 in diameter
Cushion
.... 1 x 30 cm/11.75 in square
7.0 mm crochet hook (for making squares), 6.0 mm crochet hook (for edging), wool needle, sewing needle and thread (to attach buttons)

How to Undo Sweater Wool

Long lengths of yarn can be obtained from hand-knit and ready-made sweaters alike, by carefully unpicking seams. It's best to start unwinding from the point where the knitting was completed, so check whether the sweater was knitted from the top or bottom.

cut off with scissors any parts that can't be unpicked

❶ carefully unpick sections such as shoulders, sides, and sleeves.

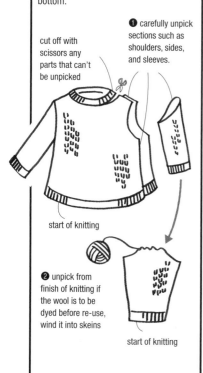

start of knitting

❷ unpick from finish of knitting if the wool is to be dyed before re-use, wind it into skeins

start of knitting

1 Preparation

Undo yarn from light cotton sweater, wash it carefully and dry it. Remove any fluff from yarn.

2 Crochet Squares

Following diagram on p. 66, make 18 granny squares of 4 rows each (about 80g/2.75 oz). Completed size should be about 10 cm/4 in square.

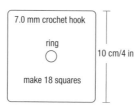

7.0 mm crochet hook

ring

10 cm/4 in

make 18 squares

3 Dye the Squares

Dye 16 squares using burnt alum mordant and 2 squares with iron acetate mordant. See p. 43 for dyeing instructions.

Do not dye yarn for sewing squares together or for edging (about 20 g/0.75 oz).

4 Shape the Squares

Place each square on an ironing board, shape to a precise 10 cm/4 in square, hold in position with pins, and press with a steam iron.

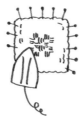

5 Sew Squares Together

Following the diagram, sew the squares together with overcast stitch using undyed yarn.

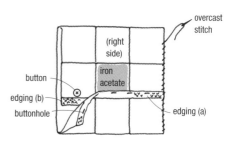

burnt alum

iron acetate

60 cm/ 24 in

❷ Sew across

❶ Sew together from top to bottom

30 cm/ 12 in

6 Crochet Edging

At the two ends that will make the opening, use remaining undyed yarn to crochet edging with 6.0 mm hook. Make buttonholes on one side as shown below.

7 Complete the Cushion Cover

Fold the work as shown and sew sides together with overcast stitch to make the cushion cover. Sew on buttons to match buttonhole positions.

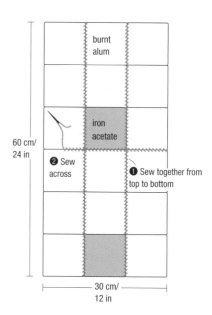

overcast stitch

(right side)

button

iron acetate

edging (b)

buttonhole

edging (a)

How to Crochet Edging and Buttonholes

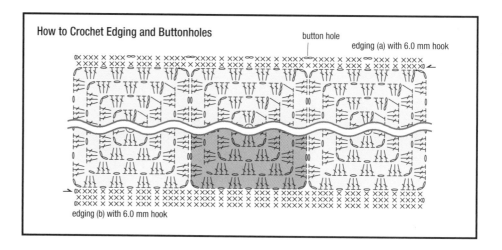

button hole

edging (a) with 6.0 mm hook

edging (b) with 6.0 mm hook

P.53 Crocheted Pot Holders

See p. 64 for dyeing instructions.

Pot Holder A

You Will Need...

Silk yarn ....approx. 3 g/ 0.1 oz
(about 8 m/8.75 yd)

Knitting wool
............................approx. 11 g/0.4 oz
(about 27 m/29.5 yd)

Mohair knitting wool
............................approx. 1 g/0.05 oz
(about 6 m/6.6 yd)

Cotton yarn
............................approx. 1 g/0.05 oz
(about 3 m/3.3 yd)

Equipment:
3.0 mm crochet hook, wool needle

Pot Holder B (4 Squares)

You Will Need...

Knitting wool
........................approx. 10 g/0.35 oz
(about 34 m/37.25 yd)

Equipment:
3.0 mm crochet hook, wool needle

Pot Holder A

1 Crochet the Square

Crochet a granny square using 4 different yarns dyed different shades (See p. 64). Make a center ring, and following the diagram on p. 66, crochet 7 rows, each row with a different yarn.

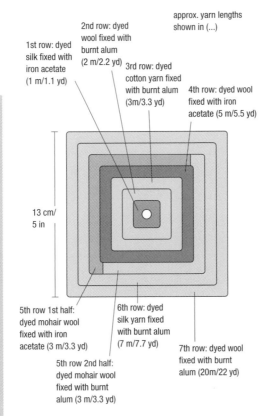

approx. yarn lengths shown in (...)

2nd row: dyed wool fixed with burnt alum (2 m/2.2 yd)

1st row: dyed silk fixed with iron acetate (1 m/1.1 yd)

3rd row: dyed cotton yarn fixed with burnt alum (3m/3.3 yd)

4th row: dyed wool fixed with iron acetate (5 m/5.5 yd)

13 cm/ 5 in

5th row 1st half: dyed mohair wool fixed with iron acetate (3 m/3.3 yd)

5th row 2nd half: dyed mohair wool fixed with burnt alum (3 m/3.3 yd)

6th row: dyed silk yarn fixed with burnt alum (7 m/7.7 yd)

7th row: dyed wool fixed with burnt alum (20m/22 yd)

2 Crochet the Edging

Using the same yarn as 7th row make the edging in single crochet. Add an extra stitch at the corners, and at the last corner make a loop in chain stitch. Finished size should be 13 cm/5 in square.

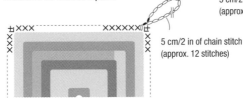

5 cm/2 in of chain stitch (approx. 12 stitches)

Pot Holder B (4 Squares)

1 Crochet 4 Squares

Crochet a granny square with wool dyed two shades (See p. 64). Make a center ring, and following the diagram on p. 66 crochet 3 rows in alternate shades of wool. Finished size should be about 6 cm/2.25 in square. Make 4.

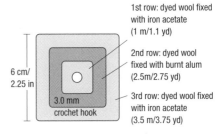

6 cm/ 2.25 in

3.0 mm crochet hook

1st row: dyed wool fixed with iron acetate (1 m/1.1 yd)

2nd row: dyed wool fixed with burnt alum (2.5m/2.75 yd)

3rd row: dyed wool fixed with iron acetate (3.5 m/3.75 yd)

Make 4 squares. Approx. yarn lengths shown in (...)

2 Sew Together

Position the squares and sew together using overcast stitch with dyed wool fixed with iron acetate.

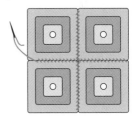

3 Crochet Edging

Make edging with single crochet, adding a loop at the final corner.

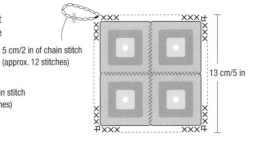

5 cm/2 in of chain stitch (approx. 12 stitches)

13 cm/5 in

How to Stitch Squares Together Using Overcast Stitch

Put the squares together, match up the corners and put the needle under adjacent stitches. Pass the yarn over the top diagonally to the next pair of stitches.

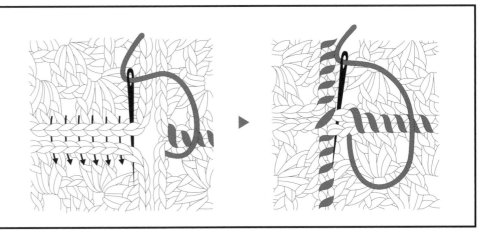

P.21 Knitted Silk Drawstring Bags

See p. 43 for dyeing instructions.

Larger Bag

You Will Need...
Old silk .... 38 x 170 cm/15 x 67 in
Silk yarn .... approx. 2.5 m/2.75 yd

Materials and equipment:
Lining fabric .... 36 x 10 cm/14 x 4 in
Patterned fabric (muslin)
.... 36 x 10 cm/14 x 4 in
Felt stiffening .... 36 x 10 cm/14 x 4 in
Twill cord (mid-brown/dark brown)
.... 50 cm/20 in of each
7.0 mm crochet hook, wool needle,
sewing needle and thread

Smaller Bag

You Will Need...
Old silk .... 38 x 30 cm/15 x 12 in
Silk yarn .... approx. 50 cm/20 in

Materials and equipment:
Lining fabric .... 22 x 7 cm/8.5 x 2.75 in
Patterned fabric (muslin)
.... 22 x 7 cm/8.5 x 2.75 in
Felt stiffening... 22 x 7 cm/8.5 x 2.75 in
7.0 mm crochet hook, wool needle,
sewing needle and thread

Larger Bag

1 Cutting the Fabric

Cut the fabrics as shown in the diagrams below. The old silk should be dyed before cutting (See p. 56).

Old silk:

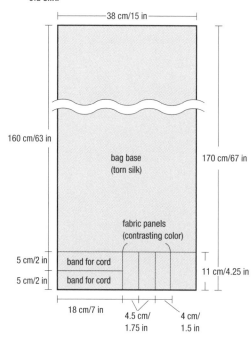

- 38 cm/15 in
- 160 cm/63 in
- 170 cm/67 in
- bag base (torn silk)
- fabric panels (contrasting color)
- 5 cm/2 in — band for cord
- 5 cm/2 in — band for cord
- 11 cm/4.25 in
- 18 cm/7 in
- 4.5 cm/1.75 in
- 4 cm/1.5 in

Muslin:

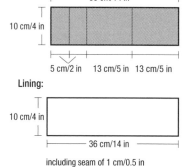

- 36 cm/14 in
- 10 cm/4 in
- 5 cm/2 in
- 13 cm/5 in
- 13 cm/5 in

Lining:

- 10 cm/4 in
- 36 cm/14 in
- including seam of 1 cm/0.5 in

2 Tearing the Silk

Tear the silk for the base of the bag by first cutting short slits into the silk alternately on the left and right, then tearing to make a single long strip 1 cm/0.5 in wide, as shown. Wind the silk into a ball to prevent tangling.

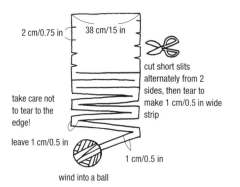

- 2 cm/0.75 in
- 38 cm/15 in
- cut short slits alternately from 2 sides, then tear to make 1 cm/0.5 in wide strip
- take care not to tear to the edge!
- leave 1 cm/0.5 in
- 1 cm/0.5 in
- wind into a ball

3 Making the Base

Starting with chain stitch, make a rectangle in single crochet, as shown. Adjust stitches and rows so that the finished size is 16 x 22 cm/6.25 x 8.5 in. Thread the end of the yarn through the back of the stitches to finish.

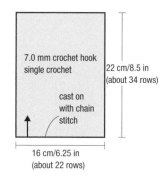

- 7.0 mm crochet hook single crochet
- 22 cm/8.5 in (about 34 rows)
- cast on with chain stitch
- 16 cm/6.25 in (about 22 rows)

Fold the crocheted panel right sides together, align the sides and sew together on both sides for 7 cm/2.75 in from the open end, using silk thread dyed the same color (See p. 56) and overcast stitch.

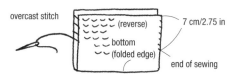

- overcast stitch
- (reverse)
- 7 cm/2.75 in
- bottom (folded edge)
- end of sewing

Fold the corners towards the center and hem down to make a gusset.

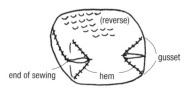

- (reverse)
- gusset
- end of sewing
- hem

4 Assemble Fabrics for Top of Bag

Sew the fabric pieces together as shown in the diagram. Press the seams with an iron onto the silk and stitch them in place. Attach the felt stiffening to the reverse. Double-fold in the ends of the fabric for cord band and sew. Fold them in half and tack in place as shown.

Cord band (old silk):

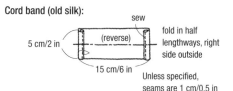

- sew
- 5 cm/2 in
- (reverse)
- fold in half lengthways, right side outside
- 15 cm/6 in
- Unless specified, seams are 1 cm/0.5 in

Bag-top fabric:

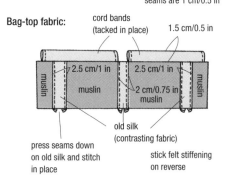

- cord bands (tacked in place)
- 1.5 cm/0.5 in
- 2.5 cm/1 in
- muslin
- 2.5 cm/1 in
- muslin
- 2 cm/0.75 in muslin
- old silk (contrasting fabric)
- press seams down on old silk and stitch in place
- stick felt stiffening on reverse

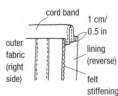
5 Make Lining

Leaving an opening for turning, sew the lining fabric onto the silk and muslin right sides together. Turn and hem the opening closed.

cord band

1 cm/0.5 in

outer fabric (right side)

lining (reverse)

felt stiffening

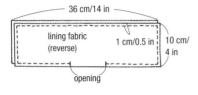

lining fabric (reverse)

36 cm/14 in

1 cm/0.5 in

10 cm/4 in

opening

6 Complete

Position the base of the fabric over the top row of the crocheted bag base and tack in place before hemming with dyed silk thread. Pass the two cords through the cord bands as shown and knot their ends together.

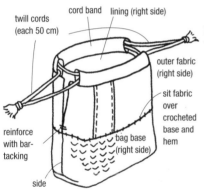

twill cords (each 50 cm)

cord band

lining (right side)

outer fabric (right side)

sit fabric over crocheted base and hem

reinforce with bar-tacking

bag base (right side)

side

1 Cut Silk

Dye old silk in the same way as the larger bag (See p. 56) and cut as shown. Tear the silk into a long 1 cm/0.5 in-wide strip. Cut the muslin and lining fabric.

2 Crochet the Base

Crochet the base as shown with the torn silk strip.

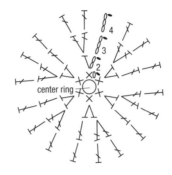

center ring

3 Make Fabric Top for Bag

Make the fabric part of the bag in the same way as for the larger bag.

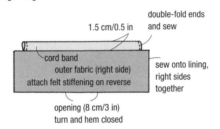

1.5 cm/0.5 in

double-fold ends and sew

cord band
outer fabric (right side)
attach felt stiffening on reverse

sew onto lining, right sides together

opening (8 cm/3 in) turn and hem closed

Old silk:

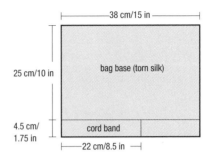

38 cm/15 in

25 cm/10 in

bag base (torn silk)

4.5 cm/1.75 in

cord band

22 cm/8.5 in

Muslin (outer fabric); lining:

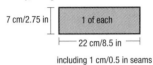

7 cm/2.75 in

1 of each

22 cm/8.5 in

including 1 cm/0.5 in seams

4 Finish

Sew together the fabric top bag and the bag base in the same way as for the larger bag. Using torn silk, crochet a chain 32 cm/12 in long to make a cord, thread it through the cord band and knot the ends together.

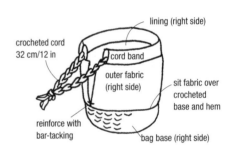

crocheted cord 32 cm/12 in

lining (right side)

cord band

outer fabric (right side)

sit fabric over crocheted base and hem

reinforce with bar-tacking

bag base (right side)

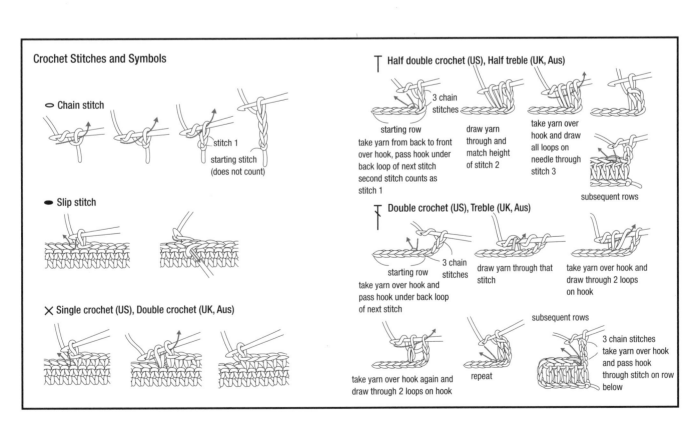

Crochet Stitches and Symbols

◯ Chain stitch

stitch 1
starting stitch (does not count)

● Slip stitch

✕ Single crochet (US), Double crochet (UK, Aus)

Т Half double crochet (US), Half treble (UK, Aus)

3 chain stitches

starting row
take yarn from back to front over hook, pass hook under back loop of next stitch second stitch counts as stitch 1

draw yarn through and match height of stitch 2

take yarn over hook and draw all loops on needle through stitch 3

subsequent rows

Т Double crochet (US), Treble (UK, Aus)

starting row
take yarn over hook and pass hook under back loop of next stitch

3 chain stitches

draw yarn through that stitch

take yarn over hook and draw through 2 loops on hook

take yarn over hook again and draw through 2 loops on hook

subsequent rows

repeat

3 chain stitches take yarn over hook and pass hook through stitch on row below

P.6 Tiny Heart-Shaped Sachets

See p. 7 for dyeing instructions

You Will Need...

For one sachet:
Linen remnant .... 20 x 10 cm/8 x 4 in

Materials and equipment:
No. 25 embroidery thread (brown)
....as required
Soap......................about 20 g/0.75 oz
Non-carbon copy paper, sewing needle
and thread, tracing paper, ballpoint pen

Fabric Remnants

It's hard to throw away remnants of
pretty fabrics, however small they are.
Try putting two together to make a piece
10 cm/4 in square.

seam 7 mm/0.25 in

(reverse)

sew up right sides
together

press seam to one side

(right
side)

stitch seam down

1 Copy a Design

Copy a preferred design of the appropriate size with
tracing paper. Mark on it points to leave an opening for
turning.

tracing paper

Fold dyed fabric (See p. 7) right-side-out and place on it
the tracing paper with non-carbon copy paper
underneath. Use a ballpoint pen to draw on the lines for
embroidery only.
If you are not embroidering, go to Step 3. If you plan to
embroider on a patchwork background, sew the
patchwork fabrics together first.

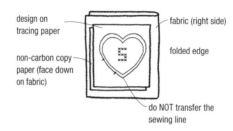

design on
tracing paper

non-carbon copy
paper (face down
on fabric)

fabric (right side)

folded edge

do NOT transfer the
sewing line

2 Embroider Design

Embroider using 2 strands of no. 25 embroidery thread.

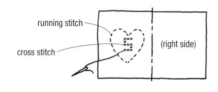

running stitch

cross stitch

(right side)

3 Sew Together

Fold the fabric with right sides together, and use the
tracing paper and non-carbon copy paper to mark the
sewing line and opening on the reverse of the fabric.

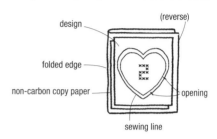

design

folded edge

non-carbon copy paper

(reverse)

opening

sewing line

Sew the fabric together following the sewing line,
leaving the opening. Sew back a little on each side of
the opening to strengthen.

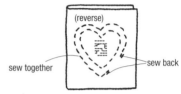

(reverse)

sew together

sew back

4 Cut Out Shape

Leaving 7 mm/0.25 in around the seam, cut out the
shape, making cuts to ease the curves.

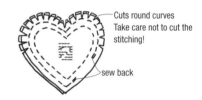

Cuts round curves
Take care not to cut the
stitching!

sew back

5 Turning Right Side Out

Turn right-side-out and press into shape with an iron.
Fold the seams along the opening and press them
down. This gives a neater finish when opening is sewn
closed.

opening

6 Fill and Close the Opening

Shave pieces of perfumed soap from a bar, fill the
sachet and close the opening as shown.

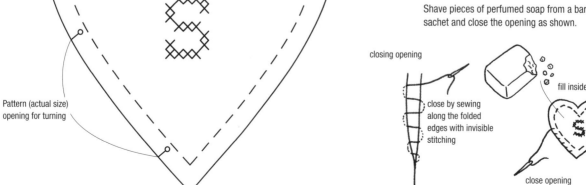

closing opening

close by sewing
along the folded
edges with invisible
stitching

fill inside

close opening

Pattern (actual size)
opening for turning

P.11 Mini Raffia Basket

See p. 14 for dyeing instructions.

You Will Need...

Natural raffia .....about 45 strands
(of which 14 are dyed)

Equipment:
Wool needle (pointed)

Raffia:

Raffia comes from dried palm leaves, and 1 strand is usually about 120 cm/ 47 in long. The strands are about 1.5 cm/0.5 in wide but they narrow towards both ends, so to join two strands they are overlapped at the point they narrow to make a strand of standard width.

narrow ends overlapped

Finished sizes: A and B

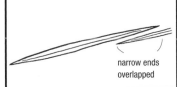

circumference at top about 24~26 cm/9.5~10 in

handle 4 mm/ 0.15 in wide x 26 cm/10 in long

passed through gaps in weave

side

base

7 rows (5 cm/2 in)

7~8 rows (9 cm/3.5 in)

7 cm/2.75 in

Finished size: C

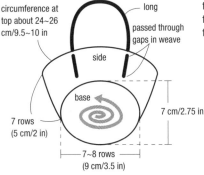

circumference at top about 24~26 cm/9.5~10 in

last row raised to make handles

side

base

9 rows (5 cm/2 in)

7 rows (8 cm/3 in)

6 cm/2.5 in

1 Plait Raffia

For baskets A and B
Take 3 strands of natural raffia, tie ends in a knot, and plait. As the strands get narrower towards the end, overlap each one with a new strand. The width of the raffia plait should be a regular 6 mm/0.25 in

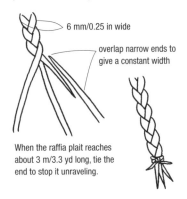

6 mm/0.25 in wide

overlap narrow ends to give a constant width

When the raffia plait reaches about 3 m/3.3 yd long, tie the end to stop it unraveling.

2 Make the Base

Thread a wool needle with dyed raffia (See p. 14) of a contrasting color. Pass the needle through one knotted end of the raffia plait, then wind the plait anti-clockwise to make a flat base, binding it in place with the dyed raffia thread as shown.

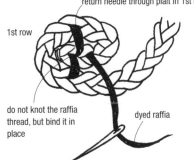

start needle at knot in center and return needle through plait in 1st row

1st row

do not knot the raffia thread, but bind it in place

dyed raffia

Bind the raffia plait together by passing the needle through the plait of one row and into the plait of the following row, to make an oval shape. After 7 or 8 rows the finished oval base should be 9 x 7 cm/3.5 x 2.75 in.

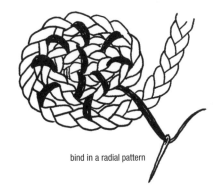

bind in a radial pattern

3 Make the Sides

When the base is complete, continue building up rows of plait from the base to complete the sides (7 rows). In the final 7th row, pass the needle over the top of the plait rather then through the middle.

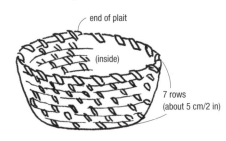

end of plait

(inside)

7 rows (about 5 cm/2 in)

At the end, undo the plait and spread the ends smoothly along the row beneath on the inside and bind them in place. Pass the needle back under the last few stitches on the inside and cut off excess.

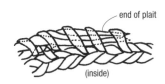

end of plait

(inside)

If the Raffia Thread is Too Short...

With the needle on the inside, draw the thread through several stitches and finish without making a knot. Start a new thread in the same way.

(inside)

4 Make the Handles

Make 2 plaits of dyed raffia 4 mm/0.15 in wide by 26 cm/10 in long. Pass the two ends between the rows in the basket as shown and finish with knots on the inside, to make 2 handles.

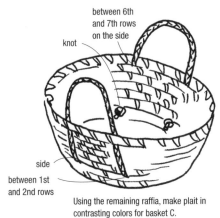

between 6th and 7th rows on the side

knot

side

between 1st and 2nd rows

Using the remaining raffia, make plait in contrasting colors for basket C.

P.22 Cloth Wrapper

See p. 58 for dyeing instructions.

You Will Need...

Linen cloth.............50 cm/20 in square
No. 25 embroidery thread (white)
....3 skeins

Materials and equipment:

Vanishing chalk, ruler/measuring tape, tumblers etc to make circles (diameters approx. 9 mm/0.25 in, 1.5 cm/0.5 in, 2.5 cm/1 in, 4 cm/1.5 in, 9 cm/3.5 in), embroidery needle

Avoid using water-soluble marking pen because it may cause discoloration of dyed fabric.

1 Draw Patterns on Fabric

On pepper-dyed cloth (See p. 58) draw patterns using tumblers etc. of all sizes. Patterns may also be drawn using the method on p. 75 Steps 1 and 2.

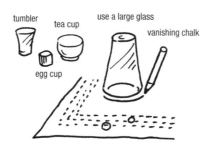

tumbler
tea cup
egg cup
use a large glass
vanishing chalk

2 Embroider Cloth

❶ Using 3 strands of clove-dyed thread, embroider round the edge with running stitch and small circles filled in with chain stitch.

❷ Use overcast stitch for large circles in the center and running stitch for mid-sized circles.

❸ Use chain stitch for the smallest circles in the center.

Recycling an Old Linen Shirt...

You may have an old linen shirt you no longer wear because of its style or condition. If so, you can recycle a big square from the back. Double-fold the cut edges and run round them with the sewing machine. The rest of the shirt can be used to make bags, etc.

back of shirt

Patterns
(25% of actual size)

To copy a pattern, use tracing paper, non-carbon copy paper, and a ballpoint pen.

running stitch+chain filling stitch / burnt alum mordant / 3-strand thread

running stitch+chain filling stitch / iron acetate mordant / 3-strand thread

For all overcast stitch use 2 strands of clove-dyed thread with burnt alum mordant.

running stitch / burnt alum mordant / 3 strands

chain filling stitch / burnt mordant / 3 strands

chain filling stitch / iron acetate mordant / 3 strands

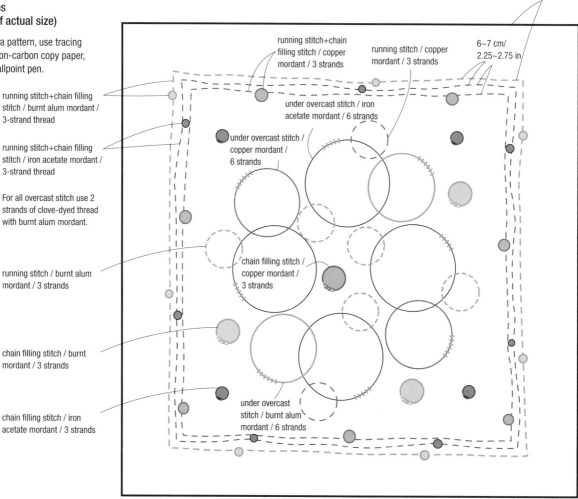

running stitch+chain filling stitch / copper mordant / 3 strands

running stitch / copper mordant / 3 strands

5 cm/2 in

6~7 cm/ 2.25~2.75 in

under overcast stitch / iron acetate mordant / 6 strands

under overcast stitch / copper mordant / 6 strands

chain filling stitch / copper mordant / 3 strands

under overcast stitch / burnt alum mordant / 6 strands

P.28 Linen Soap Bag

See p. 29 for dyeing instructions.

You Will Need...

For one bag:
Fabric remnant (100% linen)
.............................20 x 13 cm/8 x 5 in

Materials and equipment:
Flax twine, No. 25 embroidery
thread, buttons, non-carbon copy
paper, tracing paper, ballpoint pen,
embroidery needle.

Alternatively, bag can be decorated with
torchon lace dyed with the fabric.

1 Make the Bag

Fold the dyed fabric right sides together and sew up the
sides. Turn it, fold down top edge of the bag on the
outside, and sew down with running stitch to make a
pocket for a drawstring.

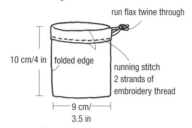

run flax twine through

10 cm/4 in | folded edge

running stitch
2 strands of
embroidery thread

9 cm/
3.5 in

2 Copy a Design

Trace chosen design (actual size) using tracing paper.

Transfer design onto soap bag
using non-carbon copy paper
and ballpoint pen.

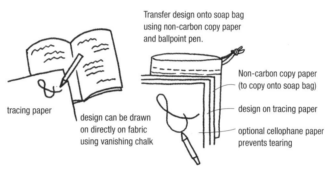

tracing paper

design can be drawn
on directly on fabric
using vanishing chalk

Non-carbon copy paper
(to copy onto soap bag)

design on tracing paper

optional cellophane paper
prevents tearing

Patterns
(100%)

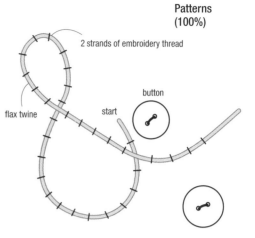

2 strands of embroidery thread

button

flax twine

start

3 Embroider Design

Place flax twine along the lines
of the design and secure it with
overcast stitch using 2 strands
of embroidery thread. Decorate
with buttons.

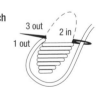

Embroidery Stitches

The stitches recommended in this book are the
common basic stitches. They are simple and can
be used widely to create a rich variety of designs.
Try mixing them in your own way for an individual
look.

• **Running stitch**

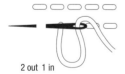

2 out 1 in

• **Back stitch**

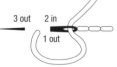

3 out   2 in
1 out

• **Straight stitch**

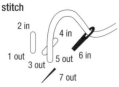

2 in
1 out   4 in
3 out 5 out 6 in
7 out

• **Chain stitch**

3 out
2 in
1 out

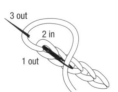

• **Chain filling stitch**

• **French knot**

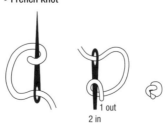

1 out
2 in

• **Overcast stitch**

2 in
3 out   1 out

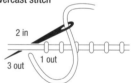

• **Daisy stitch**

3 out
1 out
2 in
4 in
5 out

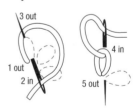

• **Satin stitch**

3 out
2 in
1 out

• **Outline stitch**

3 out
1 out
2 in

P.30 Single Rose Corsage

See p. 31 for dyeing instructions.

You Will Need...

Silk organdie ......90 cm/35.5 in square

Materials and equipment:
Double sided adhesive felt stiffening
..............................4 cm/1.5 in square
Sewing needle and thread, safety pin
(27 mm/1 in), adhesive, iron

If you're using different fabric:

- See the quantities guide below for materials other than organdie.
- Cotton or linen will dye a paler color.

Proportional to weight of fabric:

Rose leaves and stems	Water
4 times	50 times

Mordant (burnt alum; iron acetate)

For cotton or linen................................5%
For silk or wool 3%
(Dissolve burnt alum in a little hot water)

Mordant (copper mordant)

For cotton or linen..............................10%
For silk or wool 8%

1 teaspoon = 2.5 ml

1 Cut Out Fabric

Cut the fabric following the diagram on p. 77. First cut the flower part on the bias, and then the leaves and base parts.

2 Dye Fabric

Dye the fabric using burnt alum mordant for the flower and iron acetate for the leaves/base. See dyeing instructions on p. 31.

3 Make Flower

Fold the fabric lengthways, then fold the left end to the front as shown.

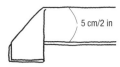

5 cm/2 in

Gather the end together and sew as shown, to make the center of the rose.

Wind the fabric round 3 times and sew in place at base.

Run a thread along the bottom edge of the fabric to gather it slightly, and continue winding it round the rose, sewing in place each time round, to form the flower.

Fold back the last of the fabric on the outside, tuck in the end to hide it, and sew it firmly in place.

fold back on outside

tuck in end

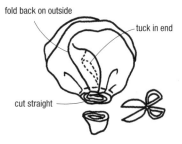

cut straight

Cut off the extra fabric at the base to make it straight. Take care not to cut sewing thread.

4 Make Leaves

Fold the fabric as shown, run a thread along the bottom, gather it and fasten thread securely.

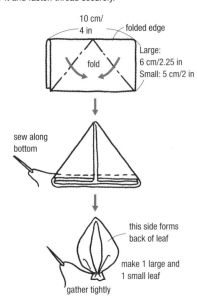

10 cm/4 in   folded edge

fold

Large:
6 cm/2.25 in
Small: 5 cm/2 in

sew along bottom

this side forms back of leaf

make 1 large and 1 small leaf

gather tightly

5 Make Base

Cut fabric for base in two, place two-sided adhesive stiffening between and press them together.

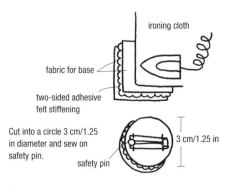

ironing cloth

fabric for base

two-sided adhesive felt stiffening

Cut into a circle 3 cm/1.25 in diameter and sew on safety pin.

safety pin

3 cm/1.25 in

6 Putting the Corsage Together

Position the leaves and sew them onto the back of the flower. Stick flower/leaves onto the base with adhesive.

❶ Sew the leaves in place

back of leaf

❷ Stick on base with adhesive

P.32 Organdie Sachet

See p. 33 for dyeing instructions.

You Will Need...

For 3 sachets:
Silk organdie
...................33 x 22 cm/13 x 8.75 in
Silk sewing thread .... 1.5 m/1.6 yd

Materials and equipment:
Potpourri.............................as required
Water-soluble marking pen, sewing needle, pinking shears

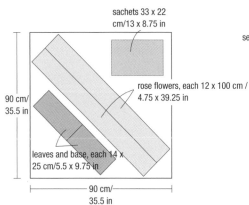

sachets 33 x 22 cm/13 x 8.75 in

rose flowers, each 12 x 100 cm / 4.75 x 39.25 in

90 cm/ 35.5 in

leaves and base, each 14 x 25 cm/5.5 x 9.75 in

90 cm/ 35.5 in

A 90 cm/35.5 in square of fabric will make 2 rose corsages and 3 organdie sachets.

Bias Fabric:

Bias means diagonal to the warp and weft of the fabric. When fabric is bias-cut it will stretch, and smooth, neat lines can be obtained for pleats or curves. The edges don't easily fray, so rough cut edges can be left without hemming. Dimensions of bias-cut fabric can vary, and so it should be cut more generously than measurements require.

Sewing with Organdie:

When sewing delicate fabrics such as organdie take care to keep sewing straight and not to distort the fabric. It helps to smooth the fabric flat on the table from time to time.

1 Cut Out Fabric

Cut our 6 pieces of organdie each 11 cm/4.25 in square. Mark 3 of them with sewing lines as shown, using a water-soluble marking pen.

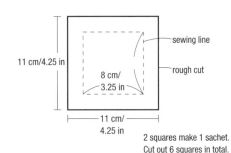

11 cm/4.25 in

8 cm/ 3.25 in

sewing line

rough cut

11 cm/ 4.25 in

2 squares make 1 sachet. Cut out 6 squares in total.

2 Sew Together

Sew 2 squares together and trim edges with pinking shears. To make an opening after the squares have been dyed, leave 10 cm/4 in of sewing thread without finishing off or making a knot.

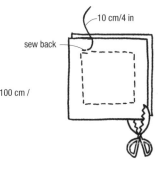

10 cm/4 in

sew back

3 Dye Fabric

See p. 33 for dyeing instructions.

4 Make Opening

Dry the dyed organdie and undo about 5 cm/2 in of the stitching to make an opening.

5 Fill with Potpourri

Fill with potpourri and close with remaining thread.

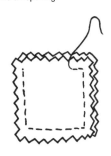

Applique with Fabric Remnants:

Leftover remnants of dyed fabric are hard to throw away. One idea for using them is to add a design to a T-shirt or tank top with appliqué. Different colors of organdie can be used together, or a print fabric can be put under the organdie. Overlapping fabric shapes creates different effects. It's fun to make something unique!

Simple hand stitching and fancy machine stitching can both look good.

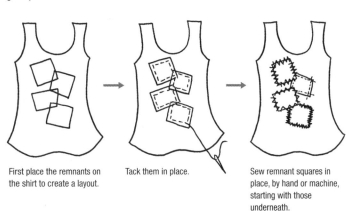

First place the remnants on the shirt to create a layout.

Tack them in place.

Sew remnant squares in place, by hand or machine, starting with those underneath.

P.36 Linen-Mix Tea Mats

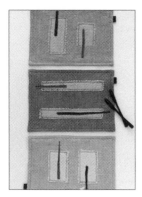

See p. 37 for dyeing instructions.

You Will Need... (for 1 mat)

Linen-mix fabric
................36 x 44 cm/14.25 x 17.25 in

Materials and equipment:
Remnants...........................as required
Sewing machine thread (brown; chestnut brown), iron

Recipe for Chestnut Paste

What do you do with chestnuts? You make delicious desserts, of course! This simple chestnut paste can be used for cakes or desserts that will look good served on these tea mats.

Ingredients:
(for about 28 30 g/1 oz balls)
Chestnuts (in shells)
.........1 kg/2.2 lb
         (without shells about 750 g/1.6 lb)
Sugar
.........50 g/5.25 oz
         (about 20% of weight of chestnuts)

❶ Boil the chestnuts until soft, and allow to cool in the cooking water. Cut the chestnuts in half to spoon them out of the shells.

❷ Puree chestnuts using a fine sieve or food processor. Add sugar and mix well.

❸ Put the mixture in a wet cloth well wrung out, and knead until completely smooth.

❹ Divide into 30 g/1 oz balls, wrap each in a cloth and squeeze tightly as shown to form them into shape.

---

1 Cut Out and Dye Fabric

Cut out the fabric as shown and dye it. The fabric for the mats is pre-treated. See p. 37 for dyeing instructions.

Remnant:

6 cm/2.25 in
36 cm/14.25 in
4 cm/1.5 in
tab
cut your own shapes for appliquéd design

Linen-mix fabric:

22 cm/8.75 in   22 cm/8.75 in
30 cm/11.75 in
mat
20 cm/7.75 in   20 cm/7.75 in   6 cm/2.25 in
44 cm/17.25 in
contrasting color (not pre-treated)

2 Sew Right Sides Together

Make a tab from a remnant and position it between the 2 layers of the mat right sides together, as shown. Sew round the edges, leaving an opening to turn it. Tacking the tab onto the mat fabric first gives a better result.

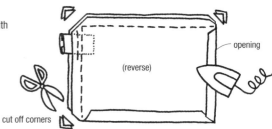

3.5 cm/1.5 in
tack in place
(reverse)   opening
1 cm/0.5 in
22 cm/8.75 in
1 cm/0.5 in seam
5 mm/0.25 in stitches
tab
(right side)
1 cm/0.5 in seam
2 cm/0.75 in
3 cm/1.25 in
Position between mat layers
30 cm/11.75 in

3 Fold Down Seams

Cut off the corners and press the seams flat with an iron, including the opening.

opening
(reverse)
cut off corners

4 Turn and Close Opening

Turn right way out and press into shape with an iron. Close up opening with invisible stitching. Run a line of stitches round edge to hold shape.

1cm/0.5 in
stitching
(right side)
close with invisible stitching

5 Add Appliqué in Contrasting Shades

Cut out shapes of fabric in contrasting color, place on mat and machine in place with zigzag stitching. Sew on further fabric pieces as wished.

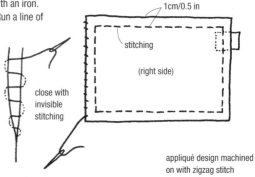

appliqué design machined on with zigzag stitch
fabric remnants

Various Sewing Machine Stitches:

With a modern sewing machine you can produce all sorts of fancy stitches without complicated attachments. For zigzag stitching, for example, you can adjust the size and the space between stitches. On a canvas of plain dyed fabric you can create a picture using these stitches as you like. Even better to change the machine thread to match the color of the dyed fabric.

P.38 Grape-Dyed Stole

See p. 39 for dyeing instructions.

You Will Need...

Silk stole.......... 35 x 130 cm/14 x 51 in

Materials and equipment:
About 450 beads, large, spherical, in 4 or 5 colors
Transparent machine thread, bead embroidery needle

1 Starting the Thread

Put the needle in through the seam and bring it out at the corner to hide the end of the thread. Make a knot where it won't show.

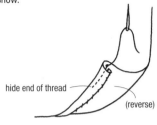

hide end of thread

(reverse)

2 Sew On Beads

Bring needle up at a point to place a bead, pick up the bead and return needle, allowing for size of bead. Sew on all the beads in the same way in a random layout.

Attach about 32 beads over a 5 cm/2 in width.

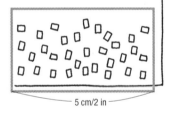

5 cm/2 in

Sewing on Beads:

Sew on loosely so as not to pull the fabric, but not too loosely, or the threads will get snagged.

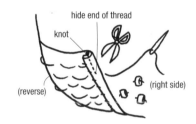

(right side)

(reverse)

from time to time, smooth the fabric flat and check the thread on reverse

3 Fasten Thread at End

In the same way as at the start, make a knot that won't show, then draw the thread through the seam to hide it and cut the end.

hide end of thread

knot

(reverse)

(right side)

Make a Beaded Fringe with Silk Thread

Use Leftover Dyeing Liquid
If you have dyeing solution left, try dyeing silk thread. In the same way as when sewing on beads, hide the start of the thread in the seam. Make a loop to start a chain, as shown.

(right side)

3 out
1 out
2 in
hide end of thread in seam

bring needle out at 3 and make second loop in loop (a) by tightening (a)

make loop (a) with thread that comes out at 1 and goes in at 2

don't pass needle through loop

(right side)

continue for desired length

(right side)

(right side)

thread beads on as preferred, with a smaller bead to finish, then return needle through larger beads

fasten thread close to bead

P.44 Red Wine-Dyed Spectacle Case

See p. 61 for dyeing instructions.

You Will Need

Outer fabric (silk) .....20 cm/8 in square
Lining (wool)............20 cm/8 in square
No. 25 embroidery thread (white)
.... 2 m/2.2 yd

Materials and equipment:
Cotton lawn print
...........................21 cm/8.25 in square
Single-sided adhesive felt stiffening
.......................20 x 35 cm/8 x 17.75 in
Lame thread, button, machine thread,
embroidery needle, iron

large yo-yo   small yo-yo
(large) x 1   (small) x 4

Patterns (60%)

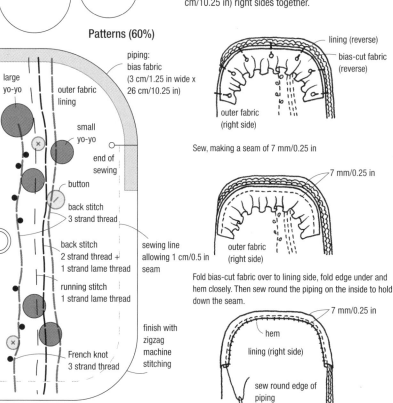

large
yo-yo

outer fabric
lining

small
yo-yo

end of
sewing

button

back stitch
3 strand thread

back stitch
2 strand thread +
1 strand lame thread

running stitch
1 strand lame thread

French knot
3 strand thread

piping:
bias fabric
(3 cm/1.25 in wide x
26 cm/10.25 in)

sewing line
allowing 1 cm/0.5 in
seam

finish with
zigzag
machine
stitching

1 Apply Adhesive Felt Stiffening

Dye outer fabric and lining (See p. 61) and apply
stiffening to the reverse of both, using an iron.

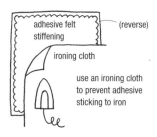

adhesive felt
stiffening   (reverse)

ironing cloth

use an ironing cloth
to prevent adhesive
sticking to iron

2 Mark and Cut Fabric

Magnify the pattern to full size and make a paper
pattern. Mark the outer fabric and lining and cut them
out. Embroider the outer fabric.

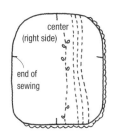

center
(right side)

end of
sewing

back stitch
3 strands embroidery
thread

back stitch 2 strands
embroidery thread
+ 1 strand lame thread

running stitch
lame thread

back stitch and French knots
3 strand embroidery thread

3 Pipe the Opening

Put the outer fabric and lining together right sides out,
and on the outer fabric round the edge of the opening
pin a strip of bias-cut fabric (3 cm/1.25 in x 26
cm/10.25 in) right sides together.

lining (reverse)

bias-cut fabric
(reverse)

outer fabric
(right side)

Sew, making a seam of 7 mm/0.25 in

7 mm/0.25 in

outer fabric
(right side)

Fold bias-cut fabric over to lining side, fold edge under and
hem closely. Then sew round the piping on the inside to hold
down the seam.

7 mm/0.25 in

hem

lining (right side)

sew round edge of
piping

4 Finish Seams

Pin outer fabric and lining together to keep them in
place, then machine them together round the edge with
zigzag stitch.

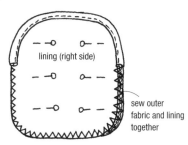

lining (right side)

sew outer
fabric and lining
together

5 Make the Case

Fold with right sides together, sew up from the bottom
to the end of sewing point, and turn right side out.

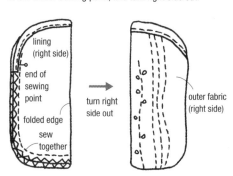

lining
(right side)

end of
sewing
point

folded edge

sew
together

turn right
side out

outer fabric
(right side)

6 Finish

Make yo-yo decorations with
remaining cotton lawn fabric.

large (4 cm/1.5 in
diameter) x 1

small (3.2 cm/1.25 in
diameter) x 4

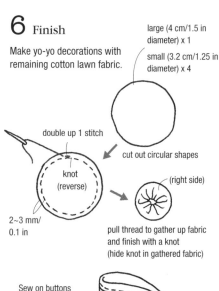

double up 1 stitch

cut out circular shapes

knot
(reverse)

(right side)

2~3 mm/
0.1 in

pull thread to gather up fabric
and finish with a knot
(hide knot in gathered fabric)

Sew on buttons
and yo-yos.

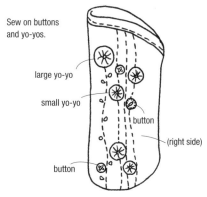

large yo-yo

small yo-yo

button

(right side)

button

P.24 Lace-Trimmed Tablecloth and Glass Holders

See p. 59 for dyeing instructions.

You Will Need...

Torchon lace (4 cm/1.5 in)
.... 2.2 m/2.4 yd
No. 25 embroidery thread (white)
.... about 2 m/2.2 yd

Materials and equipment:
Kitchen towel
.... 65 cm/26 in square
Glasses
... 2 x base about 5.5 cm/2.25 in diameter
Tacking thread, embroidery needle
Glasses should be cylindrical, without greatly widening from base

1 Cut Out the Cloth

Cut the kitchen cloth into 4 as shown and machine the rough edges with zigzag stitch.

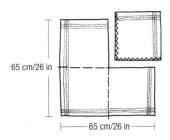

65 cm/26 in

65 cm/26 in

2 Sew On Lace

Position dyed lace (See p. 59) between cloth sections, overlapping at center, and after tacking in place, sew on using 1 strand of embroidery thread and half back stitch. Take care to keep a constant width between the sections of cloth.

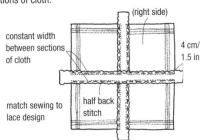

(right side)

constant width between sections of cloth

4 cm/ 1.5 in

match sewing to lace design

half back stitch

3 Finish Edge of Lace

Fold in the ends of the lace on the reverse side, cut off any excess, and hem.

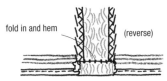

fold in and hem

(reverse)

Using Leftover Lace 2 glass holders

Sew 2 strips of lace together, fit round glass and sew ends together to make a cylinder. Make the base by running a thread round one end and pulling it tight.

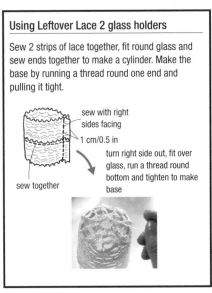

sew with right sides facing

1 cm/0.5 in

turn right side out, fit over glass, run a thread round bottom and tighten to make base

sew together

P.50 Bread Wrapper from Linen Handkerchief

See p. 57 for dyeing instructions.

You Will Need...

Linen handkerchief
.... 30 cm/12 in square
Rayon ribbon (7 mm/0.25 in)
.... 140 cm/1.5 yd
No. 25 embroidery thread
.... about 1 m/1.1 yd

Materials and equipment:
Linen fabric
.... 70 x 35 cm/27.5 x 13.75 in
Single-sided adhesive stiffening (for fine knits) .. 70 x 35 cm/27.5 x 13.75 in
Sewing machine thread, iron

1 Cut Linen Fabric

Cut linen fabric into 2 pieces 35 cm/12 in square, cut stiffening and press it on reverse side of both pieces.

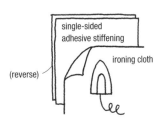

single-sided adhesive stiffening

ironing cloth

(reverse)

2 Sew on Handkerchief

Position dyed handkerchief (See p. 57) in center of right side of one linen square, sew in place, and attach ribbons at 4 corners as shown.

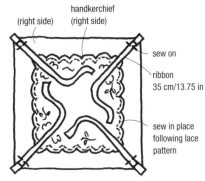

handkerchief
(right side)   (right side)

sew on

ribbon 35 cm/13.75 in

sew in place following lace pattern

3 Sew Together Two Squares

With right sides facing, sew together the two fabric squares around the edge, leaving an opening for turning.

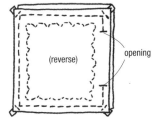

(reverse)

opening

4 Turn Right Side Out

Turn right side out, press into shape with an iron, and close up opening.

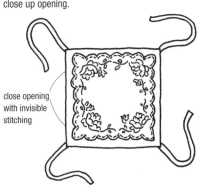

close opening with invisible stitching

81

P.46 Remaking an Old Aran Sweater

See p. 47 for dyeing instructions.

For the bag:

You Will Need...
Aran sweater .... 1 sleeve
Lining fabric (cotton print)
.... 45 x 25 cm/18 x 10 in

Materials and equipment:
Leather cord
..... 2 x width of opening + 18 cm/10 in
Machine thread, sewing needle and
thread

For the hat:

You Will Need...
Aran sweater ..... turtle collar and 1 cuff

Materials and equipment:
Strong sewing thread, wool needle

For the mini tote:

You Will Need...
Aran sweater .... 1 sleeve
Felt .... 30 x 5 cm/12 x 2 in
Lining fabric (cotton print)
.... 30 x 3 cm/12 x 1.25 in

Materials and equipment:
Linen thread (dark brown), sewing
needle and thread

Bag

1 Cut Out Sweater and Fabric

Cut off 1 sleeve of the sweater and measure the
circumference of the opening (A). Cut out the lining
fabric to match the size of the sleeve (see diagram)

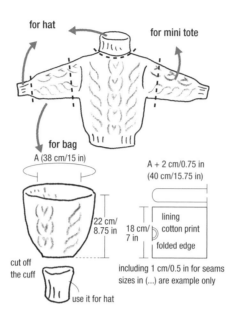

for hat

for mini tote

for bag

A (38 cm/15 in)

22 cm/8.75 in

cut off the cuff

use it for hat

A + 2 cm/0.75 in
(40 cm/15.75 in)

18 cm/7 in

lining
cotton print
folded edge

including 1 cm/0.5 in for seams
sizes in (...) are example only

2 Dye Sweater and Fabric

See p. 47 for dyeing instructions.

3 Make Bag and Lining

To make the bag, run a thread round the opening where
the cuff has been cut off and draw closed to form the
base.

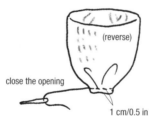

(reverse)

close the opening

1 cm/0.5 in

Fold the lining fabric with right side inside, and sew up
sides and end, leaving an opening to turn it. Turn it right
side out.

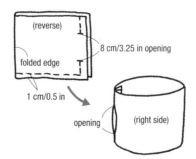

(reverse)

folded edge

8 cm/3.25 in opening

1 cm/0.5 in

opening

(right side)

4 Sew Bag and Lining Together

Fit lining inside bag with right sides facing, and sew
them together around the top with a 1 cm/0.5 in seam.

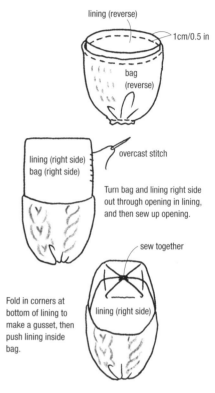

lining (reverse)

1cm/0.5 in

bag
(reverse)

lining (right side)
bag (right side)

overcast stitch

Turn bag and lining right side
out through opening in lining,
and then sew up opening.

sew together

Fold in corners at
bottom of lining to
make a gusset, then
push lining inside
bag.

lining (right side)

5 Lower Seam Inside

Lower seam where lining is attached to bag by
2 cm/0.75 in on the inside, and machine in place to
make a channel for the cord. Hand-stitch the seam
in place on the outside.

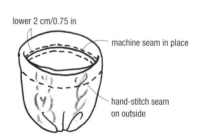

lower 2 cm/0.75 in

machine seam in place

hand-stitch seam
on outside

6 Insert Cord

Make holes in the knit of the bag on opposite sides,
pass the leather cords through the channel as shown,
and tie their ends together.

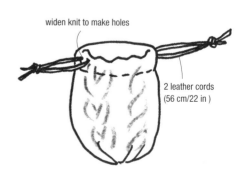

widen knit to make holes

2 leather cords
(56 cm/22 in)

1 Cut Out from Sweater

Use the turtle neck collar (undyed) and a cuff (dyed and left over from bag).

2 Make a Pompom

After dyeing the cuff, run a thread through the sleeve side and draw it together. Then pull the seam down on the inside.

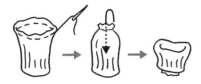

3 Make Hat

Carefully pick up the stitches where turtle neck collar was cut off and run a strong thread through them, going round twice. Draw the opening together, fitting round the pompom. Stitch the pompom to inside of hat.

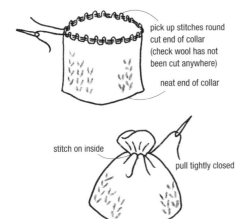

pick up stitches round cut end of collar (check wool has not been cut anywhere)

neat end of collar

stitch on inside

pull tightly closed

1 Cut Out Sweater and Fabric

Cut off a sleeve from the Aran sweater, and dye it together with felt and cotton print (See p. 47). While dyeing the sweater part, shrink it to felt the wool.

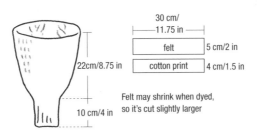

30 cm/ 11.75 in	
felt	5 cm/2 in
cotton print	4 cm/1.5 in

22cm/8.75 in

10 cm/4 in

Felt may shrink when dyed, so it's cut slightly larger

2 Sew Base

Turn sleeve inside out, and sew across top of cuff in back stitch to make the base of the bag. Leave cut end of sleeve as it is.

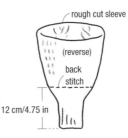

rough cut sleeve

(reverse)

back stitch

12 cm/4.75 in

3 Attach the Handle

Cut out felt and cotton print as shown in diagram below, fold felt over printed fabric both sides and sew down. Then sew onto sides of bag.

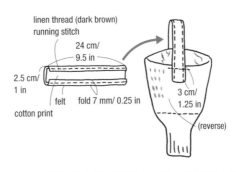

linen thread (dark brown) running stitch

24 cm/ 9.5 in

2.5 cm/ 1 in

felt fold 7 mm/ 0.25 in

cotton print

3 cm/ 1.25 in

(reverse)

4 Add Loop and Tag

Fold remaining cotton print in half and machine it with zigzag stitch to make a loop. Pass the ends of the loop through the side of the bag as shown and knot together.

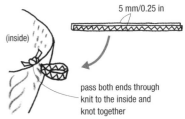

5 mm/0.25 in

(inside)

pass both ends through knit to the inside and knot together

Embroider remaining felt with linen thread, and use the same thread to make a loop. Fold the felt in two, sew round the edge and cut off any excess.

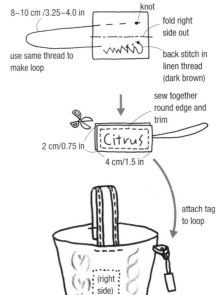

8~10 cm /3.25~4.0 in

knot

fold right side out

use same thread to make loop

back stitch in linen thread (dark brown)

sew together round edge and trim

2 cm/0.75 in

Citrus

4 cm/1.5 in

attach tag to loop

(right side)

makes pocket inside

Felting Wool

Wool will shrink if subjected to a sudden change of temperature, friction or strong detergent. Recycling an Aran sweater this way takes advantage of this, and the wool after dyeing has a different texture.

The secret is in temperatures for dyeing and rinsing. The greater the difference in temperature the more likely the wool to shrink, so the desired finish must be considered before dyeing.

Alternatively, the wool can be rubbed in hot water and soap, or washed in a washing machine, or a specialist needle can be used. There are various methods of felting to suit different materials and purposes.

• **Hat:**
The turtle neck collar is not dyed, so the wool has not been shrunk and the stitches can easily be picked up. It contrasts nicely with the dyed and felted pompom.

• **Bag:**
The dyeing solution is cooled before the wool is rinsed with water, so the wool does not shrink so much, and the softness of the Aran knit is preserved with light felting.

• **Mini tote:**
The sleeve is dyed in hot solution and then rinsed with cold water, and the temperature difference felts the wool. The wool shrinks so much that the stitches won't come unpicked, so the top edge of the tote does not have to be finished.

P.48 Scarf Knitted from Layer-Dyed Wool

See p. 49 for dyeing instructions.

You Will Need…

Wool (pale blue) .... 2 balls (80 g)

Materials, equipment:
Pair of no. 8 knitting needles, wool needle

1 Dye the Wool

Bind the wool tightly with plastic tape before dyeing (See p. 49 for details). To create contrasting shades, dye a second time with more wool bound with tape.

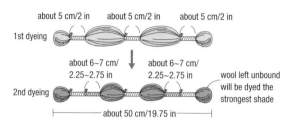

about 5 cm/2 in   about 5 cm/2 in   about 5 cm/2 in

1st dyeing

about 6~7 cm/ 2.25~2.75 in   about 6~7 cm/ 2.25~2.75 in   wool left unbound will be dyed the strongest shade

2nd dyeing

about 50 cm/19.75 in

2 Knitting the Scarf

Cast on 31 stitches. Knitting 2 stitches at beginning and end of each row, continue in single rib until 60 cm/24 in of the wool remains. Cast off.

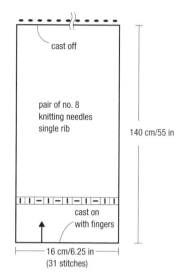

cast off

pair of no. 8 knitting needles single rib

140 cm/55 in

cast on with fingers

16 cm/6.25 in
(31 stitches)

Basics of Knitting

Usual method of casting on:

Wind wool round the fingers and insert needle as shown by the arrow.

Pull up loop with needle, then put needle under wool by forefinger and draw through as shown.

Release wool from thumb.

Tighten the loop on the needle.

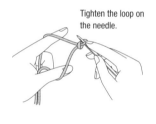

With the needle, pick up wool around thumb as shown by the arrow.

Draw wool round forefinger through loop between needle and thumb, as shown.

Release wool from thumb.

Continue to cast on required stitches. (Counted as first knit row)

Pick up wool with thumb and tighten new loop on needle.

| **Knit stitch:** |

Leaving wool at back, insert right needle as shown into next stitch from front to back.

Wind wool round right needle, and draw through to front.

That makes a knit stitch.

● **Casting off:**

pass 1st stitch over 2nd

Knit 2

With left needle, pass 1st stitch over 2nd

| **Purl stitch:** |

With wool at front, insert right needle into next stitch as shown from back to front.

Wind wool round right needle and draw it through to back.

That makes a purl stitch

Continue to knit 1 and pass stitch behind over new stitch

At end of row, pass wool through last stitch and tighten.

P.51 Felt Accessory Case

See p. 62 for dyeing instructions.

Accessory Case

You Will Need...
Felt (40% wool, 60% rayon)
.... 10 x 24 cm/4 x 9.5 in
Knitting wool...................... 4 m/4.4 yd

Materials and equipment:
Bead (5 mm/0.25 in diameter), bead
button (about 12 x 7 mm/0.5 x 0.25
in), wool needle (sharp ended)

Gift-Wrap Bag

You Will Need...
Gauze (100% cotton)
............jar circumference + 5 cm/
      2 in, jar height + 12 cm/4.75 in
Crepe *washi* paper
.... 2.5 x 5.5 cm/1 x 2.25 in
Kite string
.... 30 cm/12 in

Materials and equipment:
Sewing needle and thread
Felt shrinks when it's dyed, so cutting
dimensions are larger than case size

Accessory Case:

1 Dye Felt and Yarn

Dye felt and wool using iron acetate mordant according
to instructions on p. 62. Dye 1 m/1.1 yd of wool with
burnt alum mordant to give a contrasting shade.

2 Cut and Sew Felt

Cut off corners at 45° at one end of felt to make a flap,
and fold felt as shown. Use wool dyed with iron acetate
mordant to sew sides and decorate edges of flap with
blanket stitch.

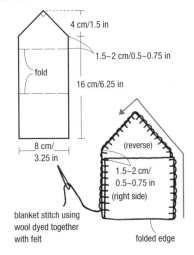

4 cm/1.5 in

1.5~2 cm/0.5~0.75 in

fold

16 cm/6.25 in

8 cm/ 3.25 in

(reverse)

1.5~2 cm/ 0.5~0.75 in (right side)

blanket stitch using wool dyed together with felt

folded edge

3 Make Cord

Cut 3 x 30 cm/12 in long strands of wool, 1 strand dyed
with iron acetate mordant and 2 strands with burnt
alum mordant. Line up and tie together at one end.
Thread the bead onto 1 strand, then plait strands to
make cord.

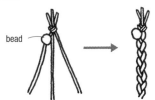

bead

Gift-Wrap Bag:

1 Cut Out Gauze

Match to size of jar, and cut out gauze.

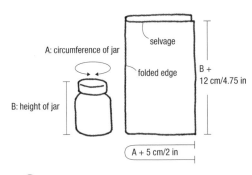

A: circumference of jar

selvage

folded edge

B + 12 cm/4.75 in

B: height of jar

A + 5 cm/2 in

2 Sew Bag

Fold gauze in half and sew bottom and sides together
as shown. Open seam on bottom flat, fold triangles at
2 ends and sew across to make a gusset.

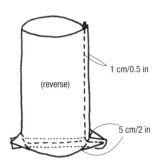

1 cm/0.5 in

(reverse)

5 cm/2 in

3 Make Tag

Dye some crepe *washi* paper and kite string with
leftover dyeing solution (See p. 62). When dry, make tag
for a message with paper, and use string to tie on bag
to complete gift wrap.

washi paper can be
dyed simply by soaking
flat in dyeing solution

hot dyeing solution

Blanket Stitch:

This is a useful stitch for joining or finishing
edges. The size of the stitches can be varied
to create different looks.

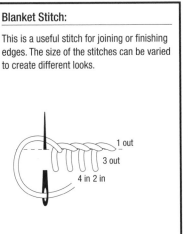

1 out
3 out
4 in 2 in

Sew end of the cord and
the button onto tip of flap.
Sew button on loosely so
that cord can easily be
wound round.

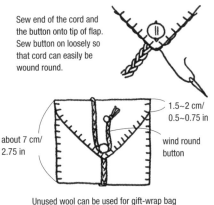

about 7 cm/ 2.75 in

1.5~2 cm/ 0.5~0.75 in

wind round button

Unused wool can be used for gift-wrap bag

P.52 Kitchen Towel Oven Mitts

See p. 63 for dyeing instructions.

You Will Need...

Waffle cloth (100% cotton)
................30 x 36 cm/11.75 x 14.25 in
Linen fabric ......20 x 12 cm/8 x 4.75 in
Cotton print....30 x 4 cm/11.75 x 1.5 in

Materials and equipment:
No. 25 embroidery thread ... 2 m/2.2 yd
Sewing needle and thread
(Waffle cloth is from recycled kitchen towel)

Patterns (50% of actual size)

Yo-yos for bag decoration
Make as many as you like

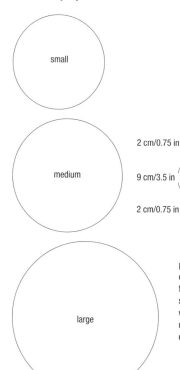

small

medium

large

1 Cut Out Fabric

Follow the diagrams and cut out dyed fabric. (See p. 63 for dyeing instructions.)

Unless specified, all seams are 1 cm/0.5 in

Waffle cloth:

36 cm/14.25 in

outer fabric | lining fabric

avoid seamed edges

├ 15 cm/ ┤ 15 cm/ ┤
6 in   6 in

Linen:

12 cm/4.75 in

for contrast
15 x 11 cm/6 x 4.25 in

├──── 20 cm/8 in ────┤

for loop 3 x 10 cm/ 1.25 x 4 in

for decorative appliqué 20 cm x 8 mm/ 8 x 0.25 in

Cotton print:

4 cm/1.5 in — for contrast
4 cm/1.5 in — for contrast

├── 15 cm/6 in ──┤

2 Sew Fabrics Together

Sew together linen and cotton print fabrics as shown, sew onto outer waffle cloth fabric, and tack on loop.

Loop:

about 8 mm/0.25 in

fold longways into 4, sew up, then fold in half crossways and tack onto waffle cloth

Contrast fabrics:

2 cm/0.75 in — cotton print
9 cm/3.5 in — linen
2 cm/0.75 in — press seams flat

├── 15 cm/6 in ──┤

place over center of outer waffle cloth fabric as shown, and sew seams down with half back stitch using 3 strands of embroidery thread.

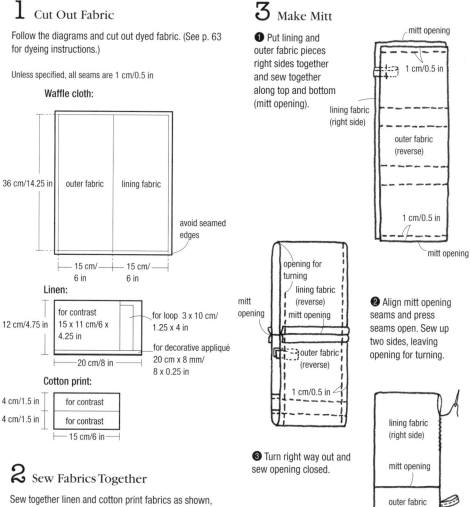

outer fabric (right side)

center

(right side)

2~3 cm/ 0.75~1.25 in

18 cm/7 in

├── 15cm/6 in ──┤

3 Make Mitt

❶ Put lining and outer fabric pieces right sides together and sew together along top and bottom (mitt opening).

mitt opening

1 cm/0.5 in

lining fabric (right side)

outer fabric (reverse)

1 cm/0.5 in

mitt opening

opening for turning

lining fabric (reverse)

mitt opening

mitt opening

outer fabric (reverse)

1 cm/0.5 in

❷ Align mitt opening seams and press seams open. Sew up two sides, leaving opening for turning.

lining fabric (right side)

mitt opening

outer fabric (right side)

❸ Turn right way out and sew opening closed.

4 Stitching and Appliqué

Push inside bag into outer bag, and with half back stitch sew decorative linen applique round mitt opening using 3 strands of embroidery thread as shown.

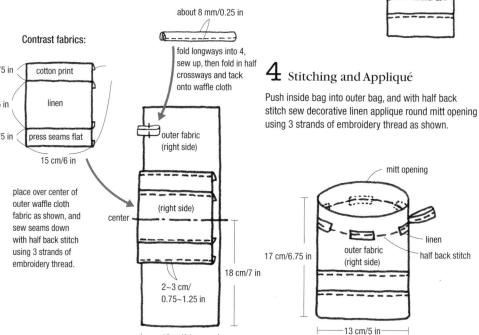

mitt opening

linen

half back stitch

17 cm/6.75 in

outer fabric (right side)

├── 13 cm/5 in ──┤

P.54 Outfit Cover from Recycled Blouse

See p. 59 for dyeing instructions.

You Will Need...

Yoke of cotton shirt 1
Cotton lawn fabric
.... 90 x 50 cm/35.5 x 19.75 in
Torchon lace (1.8 cm/0.75 in)
.... 2 m/2.2 yd

Materials and equipment:
Buttons, sewing machine thread

1 Cut out yoke of blouse saving design. Use a sewing machine to finish cut edges with zigzag stitching.

2 Cut out cotton lawn to fit hanger size, as shown.

3 Sew shirt yoke onto cotton lawn and finish the two sides with French seams.

4 Dye together with lace (See p. 57).

5 Double-fold bottom edge and hem. Sew lace along seams where yoke meets cotton lawn and along hem.

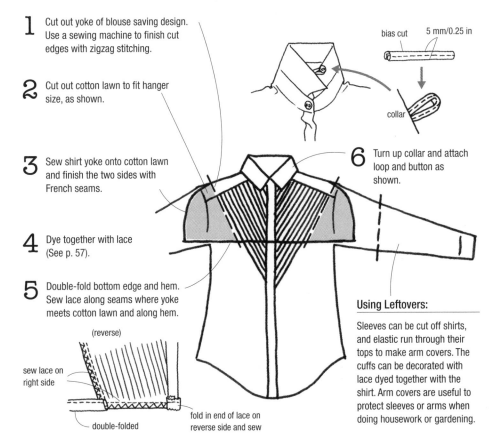

6 Turn up collar and attach loop and button as shown.

(reverse)

sew lace on right side

double-folded

fold in end of lace on reverse side and sew in place

Using Leftovers:

Sleeves can be cut off shirts, and elastic run through their tops to make arm covers. The cuffs can be decorated with lace dyed together with the shirt. Arm covers are useful to protect sleeves or arms when doing housework or gardening.

P.55 Bag from Recycled Blouse

See p. 57 for dyeing instructions.

You Will Need...

Parts of blouse
.... 2 x 40 x 50 cm/15.75 x 20 in

Materials and equipment:
Fabric for handles
.... 2 x 38 x 8 cm/15 x 3.25 in
Fabric for band
.... 8 cm/3.25 in wide x
                circumference of opening
Lining ..... same size as parts of blouse
Cotton print............ 20 x 15 cm/8 x 6 in
Tiny beads .... as required
Linen sewing thread (dark brown) and needle
This pattern takes the lining from the same blouse, but if there is insufficient fabric, use a different fabric for the lining.

1 Unpick seams of blouse, and dye 2 sleeves and other needed parts (about 50 g). See p. 57 for dyeing instructions. Dye the lining in the same way.

2 The 2 sleeves are used for outer fabric of bag. Insert tucks to shape bag opening, put right sides together and sew 2 sleeves together round sides and base. Make lining the same way.

3 Fold handle fabric longwise into four, and sew down both sides. Make 2 handles.

4 Turn outer bag right side out, insert lining, position handles and attach band.

5 Make yo-yos from printed cotton (See p. 86 for patterns and p. 80 for instructions), and sew beads round their edges. Use linen hand sewing thread to attach them to a handle.

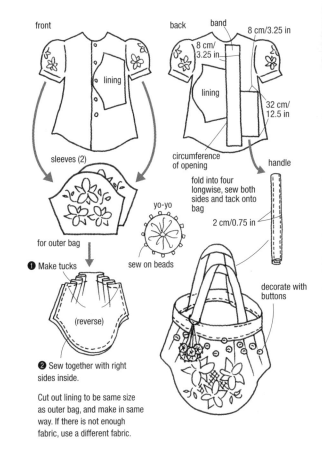

87

Profile

SETSUKO ISHII

Ms Ishii worked for some years as a designer for an apparel maker before becoming a free-lance designer. She developed an interest in dyeing with herbs while working on creative ideas for fashion and crafts pages of women's magazines. She has since promoted dyeing from all types of source materials, and has appeared on NHK and other Japanese TV stations with imaginative and enjoyable ideas for home dyeing and handicrafts. She has published two books in Japanese on home dyeing.

Dyes from Kitchen Produce:
Easy projects to make at home

First designed and published in Japan in 2009
by Graphic-sha Publishing Co., Ltd.
1-14-17 Kudan-kita, Chiyoda-ku,
Tokyo 102-0073 Japan

English edition published in Australia in 2010 by
The Images Publishing Group Pty Ltd
ABN 89 059 734 431
6 Bastow Place, Mulgrave, Victoria 3170, Australia
Tel: +61 3 9561 5544 Fax: +61 3 9561 4860
books@imagespublishing.com
www.imagespublishing.com

National Library of Australia Cataloguing-in-Publication entry:

Author:	Ishii, Setsuko.
Title:	Dyes from Kitchen Produce: Easy projects to make at home by Setsuko Ishii.
Edition:	1st ed.
ISBN:	9781864704105 (pbk.)
Subjects:	Dyes and dyeing, Domestic. Dyes and dyeing—Environmental aspects. Dyes and dyeing—Equipment and supplies. Handicraft.
Dewey Number:	667.26

IMAGES has included on its website a page for special notices
in relation to this and its other publications. Please visit
www.imagespublishing.com.

Planning:	Setsuko Ishii
Design and production:	Setsuko Ishii
Photography:	Makoto Shimomura
Book design:	CRK design (Chiaki Kitaya, Kuma Imamura), Yoko Mizutani
Illustration:	CRK design (Kumiko Yajima, Noriko Yoshiue)
English layout:	Shinichi Ishioka
English translation:	Sue Herbert
Production:	Kumiko Sakamoto (Graphic-sha Publishing Co., Ltd.)
Editor:	Beth Browne (Images Publishing)
Printed in China by:	Everbest Printing Co., Ltd.